The People's Palace Book of

GLASGOW

The People's Palace Book of GLASGOW

MAINSTREAM
PUBLISHING

EDINBURGH AND LONDON

First published in Great Britain in 1998 by
MAINSTREAM PUBLISHING COMPANY (EDINBURGH) LTD
7 Albany Street
Edinburgh EH1 3UG

ISBN 184018 068 4

A catalogue record for this book is available from the British Library

Typeset in Sabon
Printed and bound in Great Britain by Butler and Tanner Ltd, Frome

CONTENTS

Preface by Julian Spalding   7
Acknowledgements   9

CHAPTERS
1. The People's Palace   11
2. Glasgow Green   15
3. I Belong to Glasgow   21
4. Glasgow Patter – Pure Dead Brilliant, by the Way   30
5. Single-End Living and Other Housing Tales   35
6. All in a Day's Work   43
7. Made in Glasgow   53
8. Making it in Glasgow   61
9. Glasgow's River   69
10. A Tale from the Trenches (1914–18)   73
11. The Home Front (1939–45)   77
12. The Bevvy   83
13. Crime and Punishment   87
14. Dancing at the Barrowland   93
15. Doon the Watter   99
16. The Buttercup Dairy   105
17. The Talk o' the Steamie   109
18. Visions of the City   111

Important Dates   124
Further Reading   128

PREFACE

This book is about Glasgow and by Glasgow. That means it's about people and by people. *Everyone* is here, from Albert Pierrepoint, the executioner at Barlinnie, to Miss Manson, who won the best dressed window award in 1921 for her Buttercup Dairy. And every*thing* is here, from the bell that rang at eight in the morning to announce an execution to the Buttercup Dairy's commandment: 'It is always worthwhile to serve with a smile.'

This book takes you on a tour of the city travelling backwards and forwards through time, letting you compare what Glasgow was like in the past with what it is like today; when a shipbuilder would work a 69-hour, six-day week while, now, there seem to be more jobs for hairdressers than welders. This book opens doors and lets you see what is going on inside: in a single-end where a family of six people lived, loved, gave birth and died; into the steamie, where the women did the week's washing and gossiped about who had been seen out with whom and who hadn't paid the coalman; or into the Barrowland Ballroom, opened in 1934, where 2,000 people could dance the night away.

This book is a celebration of Glasgow and its people but it is also a celebration of a hundred years of the People's Palace, a museum established with the hope that it would become 'a palace of pleasure and imagination around which the people may place their affections and which may give them a home on which their memory may rest'. Though we talk now of people rather than *the* people, the ambition for this museum remains the same. Though we now do things differently in museums – since the People's Palace was founded, television, computers and international communications have totally transformed our world – still people's need for museums hasn't gone away. They are places where we can learn about the past, understand what is happening today and glimpse what the future could bring. They are, above all, places where we can meet, express thoughts and feelings and communicate with each other. They are extensions of the public domain, where people can let their imaginations wander and discover a sense of identity.

If we have managed, as we hope, to provide in this book and in our new displays in the museum a home for memory and a place for the imagination, then that is the best tribute we could possibly make to the People's Palace and to the city itself.

JULIAN SPALDING
DIRECTOR, GLASGOW MUSEUMS

ACKNOWLEDGEMENTS

This book and the exhibition it is based on are the results of the work of many more people than the authors. Though it is invidious to single out individuals we feel we must thank the following colleagues, past and present, who have contributed so much to the development of the People's Palace's new displays: Victoria Allan, Reg Archer, Margo Asken, Frank Beattie, Alan Butler, Steven Carlin, Joe Cherrie, Keith Dalkin, Ann Devlin, Jim Dunn, Lawrence Fitzgerald, Jem Fraser, Ken Gibb, Alison Gray, Elspeth King, Louise King, Fiona Liddell, Fiona MacDonald, Pamela MacMahon, Judy Mead, Maire Noonan, Linda O'Neill, Andrew Pollock, Irene Pyle, Pauline Ramsay, John Robertson, Marie Stumpff, Jim Wilson, Robert Wright and his highly skilled team, and the front of house staff who have given invaluable advice on what is interesting for the public. Ann Murray (Chief Executive's Department), Gordon Ferguson and John Grierson (Property Services Department) and Andy Worrall (Parks Department) have also helped make the whole project possible.

We would like to thank in addition a variety of advisers, especially Nick Morgan, formerly of Glasgow University; Joe Fisher, formerly of the Glasgow Room; and Andrew Jackson, Glasgow City Archivist. We have had help also from Martin Bellamy, who contributed the chapter on the Clyde, and Tony Butler, Emma Chaplin, Catriona Finlayson, Carol Henderson, Marie Logie, Katherine MacDonald, Jennifer McCarthy, Jane Sarre and Valerie Wardlaw. Responsibility for any errors of fact or interpretation of course lies with us.

The refurbishment of the building and the redisplay of the collection cost in total £1.2 million, of which Glasgow City Council contributed about one third. The rest came from the European Regional Development Fund, the Heritage Lottery Fund, the Wolfson Foundation and the TSB Foundation, to all of whom we are deeply grateful. The Glasgow Art Galleries and Museums Association has generously contributed to the cost of producing this book.

Finally, we would like to thank the staff of the Barrowland for their co-operation in developing the display. The staff of Richard Fowler Associates, who designed some of the new displays, and Silver Knight, who produced them, were a pleasure to work with. Above all we would like to thank the people of Glasgow who have made the exhibitions possible with generous donations, and by lending objects and photographs and sharing their memories with us.

LIZ CARNEGIE, HARRY DUNLOP,
SUSAN JEFFREY, MARK O'NEILL (EDITOR)
GLASGOW MUSEUMS

The Winter Gardens have always been a popular venue for all sorts of events, such as this concert of the Orpheus Choir, 1901.

CHAPTER 1

THE PEOPLE'S PALACE

The People's Palace, Glasgow's much loved history museum, was opened by Lord Rosebery on the 22nd of January, 1898. He hoped it would become 'a palace of pleasure and imagination around which the people may place their affections and which may give them a home on which their memory may rest'.

Glasgow Herald, 24 January 1898

The idea of 'palaces for the people' was discussed from the mid-nineteenth century onwards. The first such building was opened in the East End of London by Queen Victoria in 1887, to provide recreational facilities for London's East Enders. In Glasgow the idea was promoted by Councillor Robert Crawford, chairman of both the Health and the Galleries and Museums Committees, who felt strongly that the city should also be involved in looking after people's cultural needs. In response to opposition to the project from people who thought that the working-classes were not interested in art, he observed that the dirtiest

The People's Palace.

people in Glasgow had not campaigned for public baths, but when they were provided by the municipality they were the first to take advantage of them.

The People's Palace is situated on Glasgow Green in the East End, which was at the time one of the most unhealthy and overcrowded parts of the city, and was considered by some of the City Fathers to be more accessible to people than other museums in the West End and town centre. It was funded from profits from the East End Exhibition of 1891 and other public money. The foundation stone was laid in 1895. Bailie Bilsland explained the philosophy of the People's Palace at the opening:

> The general idea is that the permanent collections to be formed should relate to the history and industries of the city, and that some space should be set apart for special sectional exhibitions to be held from time to time. While primarily serving as a conservatory and a place of attraction during the shorter days, the Winter Garden portion has been designed and arranged to serve also as a hall where musical performances can be given to large audiences. One element of originality in the way of municipal enterprise that can be claimed for this institution lies in the combination, practically under one roof, of a museum, picture gallery, winter garden and music hall. So far as we are aware, no municipality in the kingdom has provided an institution combining all these features.

Glasgow Herald, 24 January 1898

The museum was designed by A. B. Macdonald, a civic engineer, in the French Renaissance style. Sculptures on the front represent the Arts and Sciences. Originally the building was divided into reading and recreation rooms on the ground floor, a museum on the first and an art gallery on the top floor.

Over the last hundred years objects have been amassed through donations and active collecting by staff. The collections reflect the changing face of the city and the different experiences of Glaswegians at home, work and leisure, both in good times and in bad. They include not only objects relating to all aspects of life in Glasgow, but also photographs and oral history recordings. The new displays installed for the centenary of the People's Palace tell the story of the people of the city from about 1750 to the present, with a new gallery for changing exhibitions.

The architecture of the Winter Gardens is said to be based on the upturned hull of Nelson's flagship the Victory.

The Winter Gardens continue to be a unique location for functions, from weddings to craft fairs. This was a celebration of the 200th anniversary of the first game of golf played on Glasgow Green in 1786.

ABOVE

Drawing of Glasgow from Arns Well, 1830s, by John Fleming and engraved by Joseph Swan.

LEFT

Washing and drying clothes on the Green near the former Templeton's carpet factory, c. 1910.

CHAPTER 2

GLASGOW GREEN

The People's Palace stands in one of the oldest and most historic parks in Scotland. It stretches from the Saltmarket at the High Court across to the Calton and Bridgeton districts, with the River Clyde to the south. The Green was probably used as the common land of the ancient Burgh of Glasgow where the townspeople exercised their right to graze their cattle and sheep. Glaswegians are very proud of their Green and over the years have defended it from property and commercial development and protected their right to give public speeches and hold demonstrations there. Most of the Green was purchased by the town council in the seventeenth and eighteenth centuries, and in 1857 it was made into a public park.

Until the nineteenth century the Green was used mainly for sheep and cattle grazing. However, this century saw many changes when it was more or less laid out as it is today. These alterations were instigated under Dr James Cleland, Superintendent of Public Works in Glasgow Corporation, between 1817 and 1826. As a result, much of the land subject to frequent flooding was levelled and drained, and both the Camlachie and Molendinar burns which flowed through the Green into the Clyde were channelled underground. Much of this work was carried out by unemployed weavers, made redundant by the introduction of the power loom. The Molendinar

Burn, which originally flowed past the cathedral along what is now Wishart Street, is traditionally believed to be the stream in which St Mungo, patron saint of the city, baptised his converts to the Christian faith in the sixth century.

A popular use of the Green was for the bleaching and washing of clothes on the banks of the river. Women of the East End could be seen washing and treading on their blankets with their dresses hitched up above their knees, an activity noted by visitors. One visitor, Rae, who came to the city in 1661, had this to say about the practice:

'The women generally to us seemed none of the handsomest. They are not very cleanly in their

'Scotch Washing' from the lid of the Glasgow Washing-House snuff box.

Football pitches on the Green, c. 1910.

THE PEOPLE'S PALACE BOOK OF GLASGOW

houses, and but sluttish in dressing their meat. Their way of washing linen is to tuck up their coats, and tread them in a tub.

The illustration on the lid of the Glasgow Green Washing-House snuff box depicts this method of washing with one woman chasing away a peeping Tom! This wash-house, opened in 1732, was the first built in the city. In the 1870s it was replaced by the Greenhead Public Baths and Wash-house. The washing greens were still in use well into the 1970s and some of the poles used by women to dry their clothes can still be seen today near the former Templeton's carpet factory.

The Green has been used for a range of leisure activities over the centuries, most importantly the Glasgow Fair, an annual holiday and celebration established by the Church in the twelfth century. From the early nineteenth century the fair was usually held at the western side of the Green near the present High Court. Despite a bye-law introduced in 1819 prohibiting sporting events and leisure pursuits, golf, tennis, bowling and the local speciality - football - have all been popular pastimes. Swimming in the Clyde was popular at Fleshers Haugh, an area at the east end of the Green. Fleshers Haugh became part of the Green in 1792 and is the site where Regent Moray gathered his army before the defeat of the army of Mary Queen of Scots at the battle of Langside in 1568. Bonnie Prince Charlie also reviewed his Jacobite troops here in 1746. In a town not in tune with the Jacobite cause, his ten-day stay was resented by the people of Glasgow, especially as they were forced to provide his army with clothing.

Over the years, attempts to develop parts of the Green for commercial purposes have been fiercely resisted by the people who cherish their traditional right to the land. In 1821 the town council gave John McDowall, owner of the Milton Iron Works, permission to develop part of the Green for coal mining. People of the East End strongly objected, particularly because of the nature of business. At the time, the Town

Council was in heavy debt partly due to the development of the West End Park. In effect the people of the East End were to lose out to the richer parts of the West End. This first verse from a period song displays the anger many felt – 'Aird John' refers to John McDowall:

Aird John since that's your name,
Let me say this to thee;
Ye'd better try some ither scheme,
An' let the green a be.
Look at yersel, John,
Is't no dishonest wark
O you, to sell the Glasgow Green,
To pay the West End Park?

The proposal was successfully blocked. Later in the century, the controversial request by the Glasgow, Monkland and Airdrie Railway Company to erect a railway viaduct through the Green was also thwarted. Suggestions in the 1970s and '80s to use part of the Green for motorway development were also made and fiercely opposed.

Over the centuries, the Green has been a site for executions, public speaking and the focus of large demonstrations. The area in front of the High Court formally known as Jocelyn or Jail Square attracted large crowds to hear the roaring voices of public speakers competing with each other for the crowd's attention. The last person publicly executed on the Green was Dr Edward Prichard, who poisoned his wife and mother-in-law in 1865.

The Green has long been used for demonstrations of all sorts, including the franchise

Rally in supprt of the Spanish Republic, 1936, showing Guy Aldred (sixth from right) who challenged the abolition of free speech on the Green in the 1920s.

Recovering after the Glasgow half marathon, 1983.

demands of the nineteenth century, temperance rallies and religious events. Indeed, when the first Reform Bill which extended the vote was passed in Parliament in 1832, over 70,000 gathered on the Green to celebrate. This right of free speech was challenged in the 1920s when the council looked on the politics of some of the speakers with disapproval. All forms of public speaking and demonstrating were banned, causing public outrage. One of the fiercest opponents was the anti-parliamentarian and anarchist Guy Aldred (1886–1963) who challenged the enactment of a hitherto unenforced bye-law of 1916. This led to years of heated debate and even rioting in the city until the old right was restored in 1932. Demonstrations and events are still held on the Green today, including May Day rallies, concerts and the Glasgow half marathon.

Monuments around the Green include the Doulton Fountain, moved here after the 1888 International Exhibition in Kelvingrove Park. This terracotta fountain, topped by a sculpture of Queen Victoria, glorifies the British Empire. The present figure replaces the original struck by lightning in 1891. Unfortunately the fountain is in poor condition and awaits restoration. Another important monument in the middle of the Green commemorates the naval victories of Viscount Horatio Nelson. This was erected by public subscription in 1806 and was the first monument erected in his honour in Britain. One of the many other interesting monuments on the Green is the McLennan Arch designed by Robert and James Adam for the Ingram Street Assembly Rooms. It was removed in 1894 using money given by Bailie James McLennan, and eventually re-erected at the Charlotte Street entrance to the Green in 1922. Today it stands in front of the High Court. Another notable monument is the Collins Fountain, erected in 1881 by temperance supporters of Sir William Collins, owner of the Collins publishing firm. He and his father were staunch supporters of the temperance movement at a time when alcohol abuse was rife in the city.

ABOVE
The city of Glasgow looking north, 1980s.

LEFT
Glasgow children.

CHAPTER 3

I BELONG TO GLASGOW

Glasgow is home . . . it is a city that has got a lot of character and a lot of character in the people as well. I think it is mainly they that are the driving force of Glasgow . . . The main thing I like about Glasgow is the sense of humour, you never get a sense of humour like that anywhere else.

John Kilmartin, artist

Glasgow is the largest city in Scotland and the fourth largest city in Britain. Today it has a population of 680,000 with more than a million people in the Greater Glasgow area. Glasgow grew from a small religious settlement established by St Mungo who came, perhaps from Fife, as a Christian missionary in the sixth century. By the end of the eighteenth century Glasgow had grown into a town of 77,000 people, praised by travellers like William Defoe: 'In a word, 'tis one of the cleanliest, most beautiful, and best built cities in Great Britain.' During the nineteenth century the population of the city exploded to 762,000 (1901) due to the concentration of work created by the industrial revolution. By 1921 there were over a million people living in Glasgow.

In the middle of the nineteenth century about two fifths of Glasgow residents had been born in Lowland Scotland, one fifth in the Highlands, and one fifth in Ireland, leaving only about one fifth 'native born'. Towards the end of the century the number of mainland Europeans – including Lithuanians, Ukrainians, Poles (many of whom were Jews fleeing persecution) and Italians – increased to about 2 per cent of the population. In the twentieth century Glasgow has attracted South Asians and Chinese (mostly from Hong Kong), and they now constitute about 3 per cent of the population. Glasgow has

been a 'multicultural' city for hundreds of years and the many different groups have contributed different qualities to the life and character of the city, becoming Glaswegian in the process.

As a human being I'm still Indian. I've lived here long. My roots are back there, my mother is there, and I still love to go back. My children are different. They feel this is their home. This is their place. They belong to Scotland. They belong to Glasgow.

Mr Saggu, science teacher in Easterhouse

SETTLIN' DOON

The vast majority of migrants to the city came from the country, which in the nineteenth century often meant being able to find work but living in physical conditions which were worse in many ways than those in the countryside. Even in the twentieth century the move could be something of a shock. Davina Matthews remembers arriving in Glasgow from Skye in 1963:

The amount of people going into the shops where everybody was moving at such a pace! Then there was the danger of maybe getting murdered. We didn't lock our doors at all where I came from and you knew everybody and it was no problem, it was a very sheltered life, so when you came down to this big city everybody was going at such a race.

Buchanan Street looking south.

Even crossing the road – I had never been taught to cross the road, because there were no roads to cross. I came to Glasgow to do my nursing training in 1963 and was not very happy about living in Glasgow, but once I got married and put down roots things were better then.

Settling down has also involved many Glaswegians in moves within the city. For generations this meant moving around the corner to neighbouring tenements after getting married. The single greatest move experienced in recent history, however, was the post-war exodus to the new housing schemes on the outskirts of the city such as Easterhouse, Castlemilk, Drumchapel and Pollok, and new towns like East Kilbride and Cumbernauld. Initially, at least, this resettlement was seen by Glaswegians as a very positive development:

My second house in Castlemilk was in Birgidale Avenue and just like my first house, it was great to have a kitchen. In the other house in Oatlands you lived, ate and slept in the same room . . . We thought we were toffs when we set the table in the living-room.

Peggy Macaulay, born 1913, The Big Flit
(The Worker's Educational Association,
Castlemilk People's History Group, Glasgow, 1990)

GETTIN' OAN

Poor immigrants to Glasgow in the nineteenth century ended up living in slum houses as they could not afford anything better. In 1831 one in six of the population was estimated to be Irish. These numbers increased with the potato famine of 1845–7. Like many other immigrants their hopes of getting on were impeded by the suspicion and hostility they encountered, as Glaswegians felt threatened by the newcomers who competed for jobs and also had a different religious culture. The phrase 'No Catholics need apply' was not uncommon in job advertisements. Other people who have moved here found a sense of welcome and belonging which made settling down easy:

Mr and Mrs Daniel's wedding, 1950s
(courtesy of Alf Daniel).

New Glasgow residents, 1960s.

That was June 1961 when I arrived at Glasgow Airport . . . I feel great about Scottish people and since then I was feeling that I must do something for Scotland. Now after 35 years I have joined the Scottish National Party with my whole heart and I would like to do anything I could for the people of Glasgow, the people of Scotland. I lived here for 35 years, I didn't go anywhere else and I don't like to go anywhere else. I've stayed here and I'll be staying here for the rest of my life.

Bashir Ahmad, businessman

Maintaining an inclusive society, however, requires constant vigilance:

> True, the ethnic minorities are, in general . . . doing well in trade and commerce. But there is no room for self-congratulation or complacency, because discrimination and racism, individual as well as institutional, and a lack of opportunities do exist in Scotland today . . . They do not think of themselves as immigrants . . . They are the new Scots.
>
> *Bashir Maan, Glasgow and Britain's first Muslim local councillor, The New Scots, (Edinburgh, 1992)*

For many migrants Glasgow has been a place of opportunity, where they have been able to overcome obstacles such as racism, religious bigotry, sexism, appalling living and working

Bashir Maan, elected as Glasgow and Britain's first Muslim local councillor, May 1970.

PREVIOUS PAGES
Drumchapel, one of the new public housing 'schemes' built after the Second World War, to relieve overcrowding in the older parts of Glasgow.

conditions, lack of training and lack of money. Exceptional examples of Glasgow's successful business people include Sir Thomas Lipton, grocer and entrepreneur, whose parents were poor Irish labourers, and Sir Reo Stakis, Greek Cypriot millionaire hotel and casino owner.

The Rendezvous Café in Duke Street, Dennistoun, was a typical small business set up by one immigrant family. Some of the fixtures and fittings are in the museum collections. In 1920 Mr Togneri came from the village of Barga in Tuscany, Italy, to work in a café in Anderston. A few years later he and a cousin took over a café in Duke Street in Dennistoun which they ran until the 1970s as the Rendezvous Café, which was particularly famed for its ice cream. Mr Togneri's daughter, Mrs Turri, was born at home in the back shop of the café where the family lived. She has many memories of what hard work it was to run the café.

> People who had been local had moved away but they always wanted to come back for ice cream . . . we even had a gentleman who used to be originally from Dennistoun. He had moved to London and once he was up seeing relations and he actually came up with a wee freezer and took the ice cream back down to London.
>
> As my father made the ice cream it was a very early rise – four or five o'clock in the morning my father was always in the café to collect the milk to make the ice cream. It was all done by hand. We didn't close until ten or eleven o'clock and it was a seven-day week. The only day he ever closed was Christmas Day.
>
> A lot of people did their courting in the shop and my father would send me down every ten minutes to clean the tables, but I'd say, 'I've cleaned them already,' but he'd say, 'Just go in and have a wee look and see what's happening there,' because that's where all the courting was done!

Hard work and the provision of a new service which added to the life of the city enabled this family to make a place for themselves in Glasgow.

Mr and Mrs Togneri in their café the Rendezvous.

LOOKIN' EFTER OOR AIN

There is a strong tradition in Glasgow of people looking after their own community, sometimes narrowly defined, sometimes including the whole city, through membership of local, religious and workplace groups such as:

• the Trades and Merchants Houses of Glasgow formally recognised in 1605 were made up of the tradesmen and merchants in the city. The organisations looked after the trading and working rights of their members and also offered financial help to members and their families who had fallen on hard times. They continue to have a charitable function today.

• the co-operative societies which were most famous for selling good quality food at an affordable price for members.

• trades unions consisting of workers gathering together and campaigning for better working conditions and fairer pay for their members.

Kinning Park Co-op Society, Women's Guild, Gorbals and Laurieston Branch banner

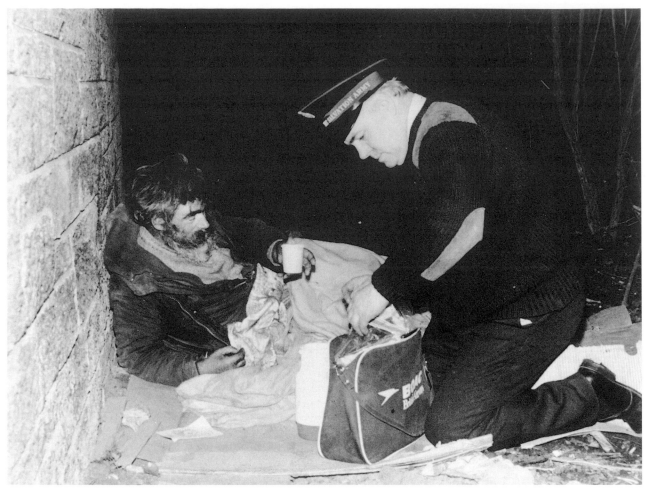

People give up time to help others less fortunate than themselves. A Salvation Army officer gives soup to a homeless man, 1987. The Salvation Army help and support people in need whatever their religion, providing the homeless with food, accommodation and furnishings. They are a Christian organisation and believe that by helping the poor they are serving Christ himself (courtesy of the Herald and Evening Times).

BELOW (left to right)
Glaswegians of many faiths enjoy the visit of the Pope to Glasgow, 1982; Orange Lodge banner; Sikh Temple, Otago Street, 1997; Muslim women studying the Koran, 1993; Hindu religious ceremony, Glasgow's West End, 1993; Glasgow Buddhist Centre, Sauchiehall Street, 1993.

THE PEOPLE'S PALACE BOOK OF GLASGOW

- family or clan societies who have looked after members who share the same name or place of origin, such as the Buchanan Society, whose chest is on display in the museum. The Buchanan Society was founded in 1725.

- people who share a concern for the poor, the sick or those suffering from injustice. Many of these were set up by people who shared the same religion or were motivated by religious beliefs, ranging from the Society of St Vincent de Paul to the Glasgow Hebrew Benevolent Society, from the Boys Brigade (founded in Glasgow in 1883) to temperance societies.

KEEPING THE FAITH

Religion has always been an important part of people's lives and many religious organisations have helped groups to sustain their culture and sense of identity. Glasgow was a predominantly Protestant city from the Reformation until the early 1800s when the number of Irish Catholics searching for work began to increase. Like later immigrants they often faced discrimination because of their religion, and group identities were expressed by organisations such as the Protestant Orange Order and the Catholic Ancient Order of Hibernians, whose regalia can be seen in the museum. Glasgow has become less sectarian but religious tensions still arise in situations such as religious marches and football matches. Football has religious connections as Glasgow's two largest football teams were originally Catholic (Celtic) and Protestant (Rangers). Although fans generally support the team originally associated with their own particular religion, the teams themselves now have non-sectarian policies.

As well as different churches representing different denominations of Christianity, including Highland churches which conduct services in Gaelic, Glasgow boasts Islamic mosques, Jewish synagogues (the oldest dating from 1878), a Hindu mandir, Sikh gurdwaras and Buddhist centres. All have affiliated organisations which sustain the culture and social customs of their members.

Garnethill Synagogue

I like Glasgow very much. It's like I've got two homes – Israel and Glasgow. Our grandfathers grew up in Russia, Germany, everywhere ... People ended up here – the boat just stopped here.

Glaswegian Jewish child, 1993

CHAPTER 4

GLASGOW PATTER — PURE DEAD BRILLIANT, BY THE WAY

In the nineteenth century Glasgow was one of the most densely populated urban places on earth. Overcrowded tenements and a dynamic mixture of people from different places generated conflict and crime, but they also generated ways of living together and surviving. As in similar cities (such as Liverpool, or New York) these survival techniques include a particular pattern of speech, whose turns of phrase and black humour reflect the intensity of city life. Perhaps this is why Glaswegians have, according to Martin Hunter of British Telecom Sales, 'the ability to create instant friendships with customers. Blessed with a quick wit and a naturally friendly personality, they talk easily with our customers' (*Sunday Times*, 31 August 1997). The result of this is that Glasgow has become a major location for telephone call centres in Britain.

That Glaswegian is now viewed as a desirable way of speaking heralds a change in attitudes, which is also reflected in the 5–14 National Guidelines for schools, which now encourage 'respect for and interest in' children's natural dialect. The recognition that Glaswegian is a contemporary urban dialect of Scots worthy of respect rather than the cause for shame is a recent change, reflected in a story told by actress Dorothy Paul about a joke her brother used to tell when growing up in the 1950s. It slyly comments on changing attitudes to 'bad' language, and her brother's naïvety about what was acceptable speech:

> You go into the grocer's shop and there is a fire and the grocer is standing in front of the fire with his hands behind his back and the wee woman says, 'Is that your Ayrshire bacon?' and he says, 'Nah, it's ma hons I'm heating.' When he told the joke he thought saying hons instead of hands was a bad thing.

Glasgow humour uses exaggeration to comic effect, as in the children's song by Harry Hagan about the heroic Glasgow cat:

> I'm a cat, I'm a cat I'm a Glasgow cat
> And my name is Sam the Skull,
> I've got claws in ma paws like a crocodile's jaws
> And a head like fermer's bull,
> Ah'm no' the kind of cat that sat on a mat,
> Or the kind that ye gie a hug,
> A'm the kind of cat that strangles rats and even the
>   occasional dug.

It also uses colourful descriptions which make the ordinary seem exotic, as in this extract from a popular song, 'Ma Wee Gallus Bloke Nae Mair':

When I went by a sweetie work ma heart began
   to beat
Saw all the hairy pie walking doon the street
Wi their flashy dashy petticoats
Flashy dashy shawls
Five and a tanner gutty boots
Oh we're the gallus Molls

Yer ma wee gallus bloke nae mair
Oh yer ma wee gallus bloke nae mair
Wi yer bell blue strides and yer bunnet tae the side
Oh yer ma wee gallus bloke nae mair.

The Glaswegian sense of humour and poetic use of language surfaces especially when people are trying to cope with serious issues such as poverty and unemployment; not as an escape, but as a way of facing the realities of life:

Many a time I think people's been right up against it and if it hidnae of been for their sense of humour they would never have survived it. Glasgow people seem to be able to cut things down to size. The humour just brings things back onto the ground. And it's no got any malice.

Councillor Agnes McLean, Come Oan, Get Aff,
BBC Radio Scotland, 24 October 1990

Glaswegians will even laugh in the face of bereavement:

Even in death we see humour. The joke about the man and his wife had been away tae Benidorm for a fortnight. Had thoroughly enjoyed it. He came back, back a day when he died, and he was lying in his coffin and wan of the neighbours came in and she says tae the neighbour, 'My God,' she says, 'doesn't Jock look as if his holiday's done him the world of good.'

Jessie Thompson, Come Oan, Get Aff,
BBC Radio Scotland, 24 October 1990

Actress Elaine C. Smith believes that along with a sense of humour Glaswegians have a healthy sense of self-worth:

There's a very big ego in this city. We've got that build them up and knock them down attitude. In the last census that we had in Glasgow, it established that 74 per cent of the population actually thought that they could be funnier than Billy Connolly, 17 per cent of the population thought that they were funnier than Billy Connolly and 9 per cent thought they were Billy Connolly. I just love that, that for me sums up the Glaswegian ego for ye.

Elaine C. Smith, The People's Patter,
BBC Radio Scotland, 31 December 1996

Part of this self-esteem is a pride that comes from having survived extremes of hardship, which brings an impatience with pretension, especially Glasgow's own:

Hell of a sense of humour the Europeans, haven't they? Ah mean they've got to huv haven't they? Making Glasgow the European City of Culture and still being able to keep a straight face. That takes some doing, eh?

Rab C. Nesbit, Come Oan, Get Aff,
BBC Radio Scotland, 24 October 1990

The story that when Queen Elizabeth II came to visit the Gorbals, a banner proudly proclaimed 'Lousy but Loyal' may well be apocryphal, but it sums up that Glaswegian degree of pride and honesty, of knowing who you are and of not giving a damn. During 1990 when Glasgow was City of Culture, a graffito complaining about the high cost of Pavarotti's visit to the city summed it all up in the phrase, 'Nae Pavarotti for the Poveratti'. Another much quoted grafitto was the addition to the city's famous slogan Glasgow's Miles Better of the tag 'than the Black Hole of Calcutta'.

For Ian Pattison, creator of the notorious patter-merchant Rab C. Nesbit, Glasgow patter is a way of speaking and a use of humour which is unique to the city:

What I do think about Glasgow is that it has a very vibrant language all of its own and things that aren't themselves intrinsically funny when said in a Glasgow way can be funny on the basis of the word play alone.

Ian Pattison, Come Oan, Get Aff,
BBC Radio Scotland, 24 October 1990

Though sometimes scoffed at by outsiders as being impenetrable, Glasgow comedians themselves have mined the difficulty of Glasgow dialect for some of their best material. Stanley Baxter, in his 1970s television series, introduced 'Parliamo Glasgow', a parody of a subtitled foreign language course, turning the humour back onto himself and Glasgow patter. He begins in a posh Scottish accent, and the Glaswegian is given in phonetic spelling for the 'learner' to repeat:

But, despite her ire, she demonstrated the Glaswegian native's innate love of poetry in the lyrical rebuke she directed at the obstinate maiden who refused to provide her with the pet bird's bowl. I listened entranced as she declaimed – 'AHADUDJI AHCANNIBUDJI AHWANT-ITRATBOUL FURMABUDJIZCLUDJI.'

The Parliamo Glasgow Omnibus, Stanley Baxter,
London Weekend Television, 1992

The difficulty in capturing Glaswegian in writing can be seen in this transcription of a story told by Johnny Beattie about his efforts to capture the response of a young man when asked on television to give an opinion on dog licences:

They stopped this guy about 18 and said what do you think. He said, 'I don't think they should, I mean, I mean, I think dugs are great company and that, the weans like them, and that,' and there's a wee boy passin' by and he says, 'I mean look at that. Ther a boy o'er there wi' a dug o'er there the noo.' And we fell about and we all sat there and tried to write it down. He rolled it all into one line. Ye couldnae get it in one line. That kind of thing is quite incomprehensible to the non-Glaswegian, obviously.

Johnny Beattie, Come Oan, Get Aff,
BBC Radio Scotland, 24 October 1990

For some writers, such as poet Tom Leonard, the use of Glaswegian is a political gesture rather than a comic device. Ian Pattison, hitting back at complaints that some Scottish television programmes need to be subtitled for English and American audiences, subtitled a commuter-belt Englishman's dialogue with Rab C. Nesbit into Glaswegian during an episode set in London.

Comedian Andy Cameron ('is that a donut or am ah rang'), whose Granny's maxim was 'I'm nae better than anybody else, but I'm as bloody good as anybody else', might not agree with Agnes McLean about the absence of malice. He recalls this classic Glasgow put-down:

I've become an actor in the High Road, you know. I got out the car and this wee woman compared me to Robert De Niro. She said, 'See compared tae Robert De Niro, by the way, you're shite.' That is Glasgow.

Andy Cameron, The People's Patter,
BBC Radio Scotland, 31 December 1996

Rival football teams, or cities like Edinburgh (where guests are said to be welcomed at the door with 'Ye'll have had yer tea'), are often the butt of barbed comments, but even these have a self-deprecating undertow:

Maybe I'm prejudiced because I'm a Glaswegian ... If I was talking about an epitaph, it would have to be 'It sure beats Aberdeen'.

Rickie Fulton, The People's Patter,
BBC Radio Scotland, 31 December 1996

Dorothy Paul tries not to compromise with language when on tour but admits that sometimes lines that get a laugh in Glasgow fail elsewhere. But it is not just non-Glaswegians who fail to recognise some of the words and phrases which are the basis of her nostalgic one-woman shows. Young Glaswegians from diverse backgrounds assimilate influences from today's global, multicultural society so that you can hear endless variations on Glaswegian, and the language of the grandparents is modified in the process. Differences in accents and vocabularies are also apparent between different parts of the city but, in the words of comic duo Francie and Josie, when it comes to facing the rest of the world all areas are united into one much loved city:

East End, West End
Bridgeton Cross or Kelvinside
Grey streets, gay streets
We love them all fur they're beside the Clyde.

We're glad that we were born in Glasgow
We're glad that Glasgow's our home town
We like the friendly folks in Glasgow
And the feeling that they'll never let ye down

Although it's not so pretty
There's something in the city
That calls ye back no matter where ye roam
We're glad that we were born in Glasgow
It's the only place that we call home.

ABOVE
*Wooden houses in the
Saltmarket, late eighteenth
century.*

LEFT
*Mr and Mrs Smith, Sword
Street, Dennistoun, c. 1920s.*

CHAPTER 5

SINGLE-END LIVING AND OTHER HOUSING TALES

A man may learn to exist without air for several minutes if he wishes so to distinguish himself; a man may live for several days without food; and clothing is not at all essential to life, but space to live on and in is an absolute necessity.

Dr B. Russell, Medical Officer for Health for Glasgow, Life in One Room, 1888

In 1888, when Dr Russell gave his famous lecture, the majority of the people of Glasgow lived in single-ends (one room) or one room and kitchen apartments, often in overcrowded or insanitary conditions. By the nineteenth century, Glasgow had become the most densely populated city of its size in Europe. This chapter focuses on living conditions and the development of housing in Glasgow during the nineteenth century leading up to the infamous slum clearances of the mid-twentieth century.

Until the eighteenth century, most Glaswegians lived around the High Street and the Saltmarket. The old town grew up around the cathedral and spread down to the Clyde. Most people lived in wooden or stone-built tenements – blocks of flats with a common entrance or close with shops or workshops at street level.

As the city grew in pace with industrialisation in the nineteenth century, the housing shortage became more acute. Three- or four-storey tenement buildings housed up to sixteen families in small flats. Serious overcrowding in the tenements encouraged the spread of diseases such as fever and, towards the end of the nineteenth century, tuberculosis. Human effluent was kept in open middens in the street. The lack of fresh air combined with poor sanitation led one medical officer to describe such housing as

'more fit for pig-sties than dwellings for human beings'.

Many single-ends or room and kitchens were as well cared for as circumstances allowed. Conditions varied from street to street or even close to close. However, nearly all of the accommodation in Glasgow was rented and tenants were at the mercy of landlords for whom made-down houses and overcrowding were a way of maximising profits. The description of 64 Havannah Street gives some indication of the extremes of overcrowding:

64 Havannah Street is not surpassed by any close in the city for filth, misery, crime and disease; it contains 59 houses, all inhabited by a most wretched class of individuals; several of these houses do not exceed 15 feet square, yet they are forced to contain a family of sometimes six persons.

W.T. Gairdner, report of the Medical Officer of Health, October 1863

ATTEMPTS TO CONTROL OVERCROWDING

Overcrowding under these conditions meant that people's health suffered. Mortality rates rose according to the number of people living in each room. After the Glasgow Improvement Act

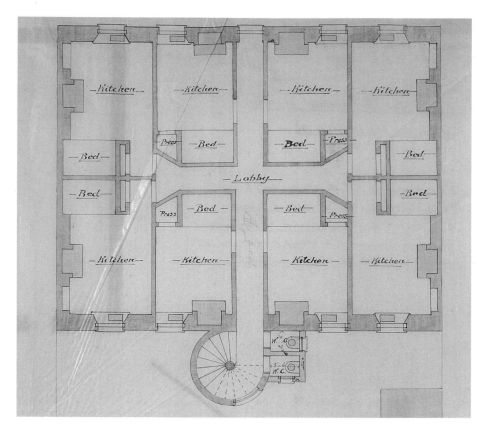

LEFT
Floor plan of eight single-ends after the Glasgow Improvement Act, 1866.

BELOW
Model lodging house, Abercromby Street, c. 1920s.

of 1866 'model' lodging houses were set up in the city to accommodate the homeless and single men who were often newcomers to the city. By 1914 there were 32 model lodging houses in the city.

In an attempt to control overcrowding in the tenements a system of ticketing was introduced under the Police Act of 1866. Tickets, examples of which are on display in the museum, were attached to each house and showed the number of people allowed to live in it. Children under eight were counted as half an adult. Even after the Improvement Act some parties questioned whether overcrowding was a reality or simply an excuse:

> Overcrowding: This where it is found to exist, is more frequently due not so much to a lack of means [wages] as to the manner in which they are spent and to the indifference that is found amongst a class of the population as to what is termed 'the decencies of life'. These people have never been accustomed to anything else and consequently think nothing of it.
> *Glasgow Municipal Commission into the Housing of the Poor, evidence of J. C. McKellar, 1903*

By 1914, 22,000 houses were ticketed in Glasgow. Six inspectors were employed by Glasgow Corporation Sanitary Department to inspect houses between the hours of 11.30 p.m. and 5 a.m. If houses were more than 30 per cent overcrowded the tenants could be prosecuted. Inspectors visited at night because beds, or what passed for bedding, were put away during the day. People would sleep anywhere.

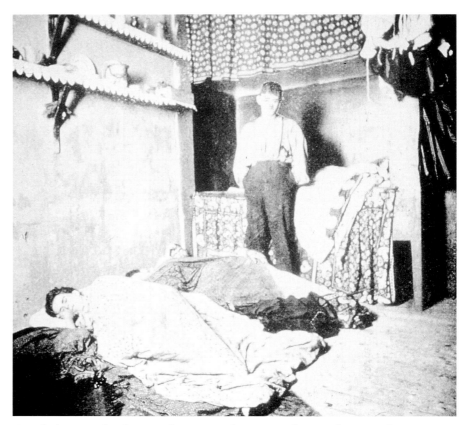

Posed photograph taken in a house in Bolton Street (later Ardgowan Place), c. 1892, shows what the night inspectors found on their visit to ticketed houses.

A PLACE TO BE BORN, A PLACE TO DIE

Even in less crowded single-ends or room and kitchens, hurlie beds would be put away during the day. Most houses would have a bed recess sometimes covered by a curtain. This bed would usually be occupied by the parents and all of the children of the house would have been born in it. The dead would also have been laid out on the bed. Infant mortality was highest in the poorest areas, as it remains today. A health visitor working in Glasgow as late as the 1950s highlights the conditions she often worked under:

> On a midwifery level many of the beds were hairy, and I mean hairy in every sense of the word. There were hair mattresses and pets as well. Often the women would be in a lovely dip in the middle and what I would do is take a dining-room chair and

literally take the seat out and put the woman's bottom on that so at least we would have a smooth rigid surface.

Children in overcrowded homes shared with men and women, boys and girls, often from different families, were considered to be morally at risk. Ralph Glasser, in *Growing up in the Gorbals*, suggests that the fear was well justified:

'Come on!' he said disbelieving, 'Yewr sisters must've shown ye whit's what? Ah'll lay ye odds o' a hundred tae one, ye'll no find a feller, who's go' an older sister, who's no' been intae 'er – aye many, many times sleeping in the same bed night efter night! Hiv ye really no' done i'? Ah'll no' tell on ye mind!'

Domestic and sexual violence meant that for many women and children the place where they should have been safest put them at most risk. They had few options to escape. The experience of a life lived in fear is expressed in the following quotation from a Glasgow woman who was over eighty years old before she felt able to discuss the matter:

I had 47 years in fear. I used to lie out in the stairs till he went to sleep before I got in the window. My family used to ask me why I stuck it. I stuck it for them. Nobody could take you in.

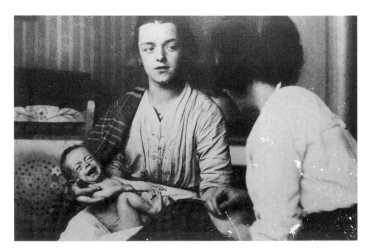

Health visitor, c. 1920s.

A GLASGOW CHILDHOOD

The moral and physical well-being of children was uppermost in the minds of housing reformers such as Dr Russell:

I wish our authorities would think a little more of the toddling 'things' who cannot walk to our parks and whose mothers have not time to carry them thither. One often stumbles over them creeping in dark lobbies, with their attempts to play at houses on the stairs. If they venture further they will only find the dead air and nauseous environments of back courts, or the dangerous street.

Children in the poorest areas had nowhere safe to play either indoors or out. Little had changed by 1915:

The children are forced out of doors to give the housewife room to work. In my evening visitation I find the children are everywhere – sitting in the closes and on the stairs, trying to play, often half asleep, on bitter winter nights. Sometimes they play in the dark, evil-smelling courts, sometimes in the dimly lit streets, and they learn no good.

Reverend David Watson, evidence to the
Royal Commission on Housing in Scotland, 1915

Even after the 1898 Police Act made it compulsory for tenements to have a toilet on every landing, the midden was still a dangerous adventure playground. Margaret Thomson, growing up in Bridgeton in the 1950s, remembers the midden fondly:

I used to play in the middens where I caught scarlet fever. It was just something different to do. Just looking for luckies. I don't know what you were looking for but you just did it. You used to always see dead cats and the boys used to lift them by the tail and throw them at you.

Thistle Street, Gorbals, October 1917 (photograph copyright Glasgow City Archive).

KEEPING DECENT

Keeping children clean and healthy remained a problem in the tenements. By 1956, 38 per cent of houses still did not have a fixed bath or shower. Small children would be washed in the jaw-box or sink; older children might be washed in a tin bath in front of the fire or range. Families keen to remain respectable were very careful to keep boys and girls apart when they were being washed, as this extract from a Govan childhood in the 1940s shows: 'Govanites were fairly puritanical about some things. Despite the overcrowding, it was rare for our boys to see sisters undressing. The women would draw the curtains over the 'set-in bed' and change in there.' Keeping yourself clean was a way of showing the world that you were respectable:

> The badge of rank was cleanliness, and cleanliness was preserved in bug-infested houses with one tap in a kitchen sink as its only instrument. The children went out to school like new pins, and there was a patch of clean air in the fetid fog.
>
> *James Bridie,* One Way of Living, *1939*

Even after houses were built with a bath the authorities doubted that the public would use them, as this extract from a report from 1925 shows:

> Do the people appreciate them and use them, because allegations have been made that these baths are used for every purpose except washing? A lot of them are used for coals and sundry articles, but you have to give them baths and they can use them as they like.
>
> *Evidence to the Royal Commission on*
> *Housing in Scotland, 1925*

This statement highlights the belief that slums were caused by the people themselves. Most people had little choice but to live in cramped conditions. A single-end was also considered easier to keep than a room and kitchen:

> We were in a room and kitchen until the death of my mother in 1914. My father took the decision to move to one of the single-ends because he thought it would be easier to look after. It was a dreadful decision because it meant you had three men in one room. You couldn't get out each other's road.
>
> *Councillor Charles Davidson, born 1910s*

BE IT EVER SO HUMBLE

After the Second World War, the housing shortage meant that people were happy and indeed proud to have a single-end of their own. For some couples who had been living with parents a single-end offered the chance of independence:

> It was smashing because when you are sharing with in-laws it is not so hot, but to get your wee single-end was great. You still had your outside toilet and your hole-in-the wall bed. That was it until we moved to Drumchapel.
>
> *Elizabeth Dawn, born 1900s*

Until the 1970s, 80 per cent of people in the Gorbals lived in single-ends. The initial efforts of the city council to build houses during the 1920s and '30s became wholesale after the post-war slum clearances and led to the construction of large housing schemes on the outskirts of the city. The move to the schemes gave people the chance to have bigger houses, but it changed their way of life for ever. For Billy Connolly, this was no bad thing:

> People say you were brought up in Glasgow, Mr Connolly, in tenement life, and wasn't there a great sense of community. I say, aye when there's sixty-five of ye sharing the toilet it kind of breeds a sense of community. Ye never get a cauld seat for a start.
>
> *Billy Connolly* Come Oan, Get Aff,
> *BBC Radio Scotland, 24 October 1990*

Many people cite the move to the housing scheme as heralding the breakdown of community life where families lived together or at least close by and everyone knew their neighbours. Mary Blackie, born in Partick in the 1910s, is typical:

> I remember a tenement where you could walk out and talk to your neighbours or leave your door open. You can't do that now. You could leave the key in the door and say, 'Come in for a cup of tea.' You can't do that now. You can't get your door locked quick enough. Oh, I don't know. I've known life so long like this.

HOME, SWEET HOME

In the old tenements in overcrowded schemes people were never alone. They lived, loved, fought, were born, grew into adulthood and sometimes died alongside each other. The intensity of living under these conditions created bonds which seem absent today. Many people feel nostalgia for the past. Today we expect to have space to feel private. Living patterns have changed with young people more likely to leave home to live alone before or instead of marriage. Many old people now live alone. Above all the most significant change is the move to home ownership. Small flats which once housed whole families are now bought as first-time buyers' homes.

Managers and foremen on a steam locomotive, Neilson and Co's Hydepark Works, Finnieston, Glasgow, c. 1859 (courtesy of The Mitchell Library).

LEFT
Housework around 1900 (from a series of lantern slides showing the evils of alcohol).

CHAPTER 6

ALL IN A DAY'S WORK

I'm looking for a job with a sky-high pay,
A four-day week and a two-hour day,
S'maybe because I'm inclined that way
But I never did like being idle!

Matt McGinn, 'I'm Looking for a Job'

In the nineteenth century the combination of low wages (compared to other Scottish or English cities) and unpredictable work contributed to many traditional features of Glasgow life: living in single-ends, the importance of the pawn shop and the 'midnight flit', when unemployment meant that rapid removal to even more basic accommodation without paying arrears of rent was necessary.

Unemployment and underemployment are not recent phenomena in Glasgow, but have been persistent problems for at least 200 years. This has been due to many factors: technical innovations such as the introduction of cotton-spinning machinery; huge fluctuations in the work available caused by booms and slumps in the economy; seasonal working, which meant that around 1900, 25 per cent of Glasgow workers were in occupations which put them out of work at some stage during the year. Workers in marine industries, from shipbuilders to dockers, and building were particularly affected by these cycles. This, it must be remembered, was at a time before the introduction of old age pensions (1908, for the over seventies) and unemployment insurance (1911). To a large extent the image of a prosperous Glasgow is based on memories of the short-lived period of full employment which followed the Second World War.

Women have always done strenuous unpaid work as part of the job of running a home. Due to the dominance of heavy industry in nineteenth-century Glasgow there were few employment opportunities for married women – in 1911 only 9.6 per cent of married and widowed women were recorded by the census as being in paid work. Though this may hide work in the home such as dressmaking, it meant a lower standard of living for many families, and pressure on children to begin earning as soon as possible. The effects of two World Wars in breaking down barriers to exclusively male occupations and the availability of modern domestic appliances such as Hoovers and automatic washing machines have combined to enable women to enter the workforce (though recent studies show that despite working outside the home, women still do most of the housework and childcare). In 1993, for the first time in history, more jobs were held by women than by men in Glasgow, many of them in low-paid service industry jobs. To a large extent this has been caused as much by a reduction in the number of men in work as by an increase in the number of women. Though unemployment is falling in Glasgow, in mid-1996 it was still 13.2 per cent of the economically active (17.5 per cent for men, 7.2 per cent for women) compared to the UK average of 7.6 per cent. The loss of

Prince's Square shopping centre.

heavy industry was a blow not just to the economy but to the self-respect of many men and their sons, who now find it very difficult to find skilled or well-paid jobs.

Despite its image as an industrial city a large proportion of the city's population has always worked in service industries – in the many shops, transport, food and drink, banks and financial businesses which served Glasgow's population. The council itself has long been the single largest employer in the city, and has actively promoted the city's service economy through events such as the Garden Festival of 1988 and its year as European City of Culture in 1990. The result of this has been that Glasgow is the third most visited tourist city in Britain (after London and Edinburgh), so it seems likely that in the foreseeable future Glaswegians with jobs will most likely be working in services of one kind or another.

GET A TRADE, SON

The traditional image of work in Glasgow is based on the heavy engineering and shipbuilding industries for which the city was famous, and this is reflected in the many specialist tools in the museum's collection. Great strength as well as skill was required to work the heavy machines

and tools, and these were a source of pride for the many men who made 'Clyde-built' a byword for quality engineering. Traditional parental advice to 'get a trade, son, it's a job for life' reflects the limited ambition of most families, though even this meant sacrifice, as boys could earn more by working as a labourer than as an apprentice. There was great competition for trade apprenticeships, and knowing someone in the works, or a recommendation from someone influential, often made the difference, as it did for Willie Galloway: 'I left school when I was 15, and I started at Fairfields in October, as a boy helper. Well I only got started as my father was a foreman, a foreman plumber. It was him that got me the job.' Willie retired as pipeworks manager in 1979.

By the 1970s this advice was increasingly out of date, as the economy shifted from manufacturing to services:

> Back then the conventional wisdom was to get a trade at your fingertips and I remember that the only thing I wanted to be was a hairdresser because I couldn't be a Beatle . . . But my mum would say, 'Oh no. Get a trade at your fingertips.' The irony of this was there are millions more jobs as hairdressers than there are welders.
>
> *Ian Pattison, writer and creator of Rab C. Nesbit*

More ambitious parents also encouraged their children to take whatever educational opportunities were on offer, though continuing secondary school beyond the minimum age put a great burden on most families. Until 1945 entrance to university was restricted to those who could afford to pay the fees and forego earning a wage. The grant system introduced after that date enabled many young people to get a higher level of education and a better job than their parents would have dreamed possible – and Glasgow's universities have been more successful than most in Britain in attracting working-class students most of whom live at home. Today cuts in the grants and the introduction of student loans and tuition fees is

Men forging metal with a steam hammer being overseen by their boss, David Rowan & Co. Ltd Engineering Company, 1950s (courtesy of Glasgow City Archives).

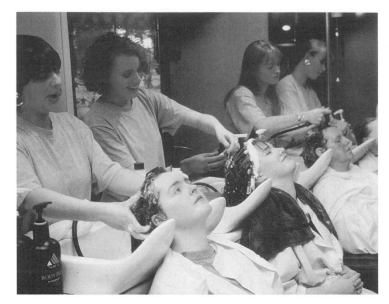

*Glasgow hairdressers,
1980s
(courtesy of
Springburn Museum).*

*Glasgow University
graduates, 1986
(copyright Susan
Tweedie).*

*Health and safety is a
concern even in
modern offices, where
back, eye and
muscular problems
can arise due to long
periods of sitting
looking at monitors
and repetitive actions,
1990 (courtesy of
Cranhill Arts).*

Welder wearing protective clothes and gloves, 1950s (courtesy of Glasgow City Archives).

Staff in Glasgow City Council Housing Department, 1995 (copyright Steve Hosie).

In the 1950s asbestos workers were not always provided with protective clothing, which meant that they suffered serious health problems later (courtesy of Glasgow City Archives).

again making it difficult for children of less well off people to attend university and college. Even a degree is no longer a guarantee of a secure job. A lot of professional work is now on short-term contract, saving employers the expense of having permanent staff.

DANGER – WORK CAN DAMAGE YOUR HEALTH!

You will easily know a chrome worker from the fact that, as a rule, the bridge of his nose is

LEFT

The Scottish Trades Union Congress banner, by Central Designs. The STUC was established in 1897 and is an umbrella organisation made up of all the trade unions in Scotland.

BELOW

Women striking at Rolls-Royce, Hillington, 1955, for equal pay for doing the same job as men.

completely eaten away [chrome workers worked with a dangerous chemical]. In some cases, where they have not been employed so long amongst the chrome, you will notice that the nose is often partly decayed and in holes.

Dundee People's Journal, *1889, 'The Labouring Classes in Glasgow, Their Conditions and their Grievances'*

All sorts of work can be dangerous, from the risk of carrying heavy weights to repetitive strain injury caused by operating modern office equipment such as word processors. In the nineteenth century the pace of work accelerated and workers were forced to work faster, and for longer hours, often using dangerous materials and machinery. In the mid-nineteenth century Glasgow workers on average did a 69-hour, six-

RIGHT
Morris's *furniture factory strike, 1986.*

BELOW
Big Issue *seller, Duke Street, 1994.*

day week. Fatal or disabling industrial accidents were common, especially for older workers, in an age when 'retirement' meant becoming a burden on one's family.

Many industrial jobs have involved working with heavy machinery and hot metal, where the dangers were more visible. Welding is a job where hazards are obvious and protective clothing has always been worn. Less obvious dangers which took longer to have an effect, such as damage to people's hearing caused by 'metal-bashing', have only recently been addressed, and workers provided with protection. Working in modern offices can also have health and safety risks. In many workplaces the use of computers is strictly monitored as continual use can cause serious eye and back injury.

Though various acts were passed in the nineteenth century to make work safer, and to compensate workers for industrial injuries, unions tended to be more preoccupied with protecting wages, and it was not until after 1945 that a comprehensive approach began to be taken to health and safety at work. Even after this date, known dangers were sometimes allowed to persist, such as that from asbestos. Workers therefore worked without protective clothing, for example in the construction of many of the tower blocks built in Glasgow in the 1960s, and later suffered from industrial diseases such as asbestosis.

UNITED WE STAND

Be the author of your own destiny. Control your occupation – don't let it control you.

Trade union banner (the Union of Shop, Distributive and Allied Workers)

Glasgow workers have gathered together in trade unions since the 1700s, to fight to improve their pay and working conditions, and this is reflected in the People's Palace collection of trade union banners, which is one of the finest in Britain. When workers have had grievances about these things their main bargaining power has been to go on strike, and special banners were often improvised for the event. When the government tried to close the Upper Clyde Shipyards in 1971, instead of a strike the unions organised a different type of industrial protest, a work-in. To prove that shipbuilding was still a going concern the workers continued to build ships despite the attempted closure of the yard. This dispute symbolised the decline in shipbuilding in Glasgow and was supported by many unions. Much union activity has successfully improved wages and conditions.

Although often doing the same jobs, women have traditionally been paid less than men. Divisions within the working classes – between skilled and unskilled, men and women, Catholics and Protestants, black and white – meant that women, the unemployed and immigrants, often forced to take unskilled or part-time work, have not had the automatic support of the trade unions. In 1980 1.1 million Scottish workers were members of trade unions; by 1993 that number had dropped to just over 750,000. The decline in union membership has been due to changes in work patterns, with more mobile, more part-time and more women workers, and government restrictions on the activities of unions, which made them seem less effective. Trade unions have also had an important political role in the city, and have taken part in many campaigns, especially those for parliamentary reform which reached high points in massive demonstrations leading to the Reform Acts of 1832, 1867 and 1884.

While unions work to adjust to rapidly changing circumstances, the displays in the People's Palace show that many workplace and political rights which we take for granted were won as a result of collective action. May Day is still an important event in the Glasgow calendar, and the parade with its many banners usually culminates in Glasgow Green near the museum.

Major Work Events

1760

Highland clearances drive many Highlanders to seek work in Glasgow.

1791

15,000 cotton-weaving handlooms in the greater Glasgow area, employing 135,000 people.

1799

Scottish miners released from serfdom – up to this date the children of miners had to work in mines.

1806

Four hundred steam looms for weaving cotton being operated in Glasgow.

1833

Factory Act appoints the first inspectors to enforce prohibition of children under nine from working, and limit the hours of 9–12-year-olds to nine hours a day.

1841

One in three Glasgow workers is employed in the textile industry. Two thirds of them are women, mostly working from home or in small workshops. One in nine Glasgow workers is employed as a domestic servant, most of them women.

1845–7

Thousands of Highlanders and Irish migrants, fleeing the potato famine, come to Glasgow for work, especially in railway navvying and building sectors. Catholic Irish discriminated against in employment, especially in skilled trades.

1851

Sixty-one die in mining disaster in Victoria Pit, Nitshill.

1861

Textile industry still a major employer, with about 12,000 people in 60 factories. After 1861 heavy industries take over more and more, reducing the number of women workers. Family incomes fall as a result.

1866

Twenty thousand workers on the Clyde strike, unsuccessfully, for a nine-hour day. First women employed as tracers in engineering drawing offices, despite objections.

1872

Education Act makes education free and compulsory up to the age of 13.

1883

The *Daphne* launched into the Clyde with men still working on board; 124 drown when it capsizes.

1884

Forty-one yards building ships on the Clyde.

1889

Twenty-nine killed when wall of Templeton's Carpet Factory collapses on weaving sheds.

1890

About 6,000 Jewish migrants, fleeing persecution in Eastern Europe, arrive in Glasgow.

1890–1914

First Italian migrants set up ice cream parlours and fish and chip shops.

1891/2

Failure of the railway strike, leading to longer hours and more accidents.

1892

Women admitted to Glasgow University for the first time.

1901
Four per cent of all women in Glasgow work as domestic servants.

1905
North British Locomotive Company employs 8,000 men.

1908
Liberal Government introduces Old Age Pension Scheme.

1908/9
Serious economic depression leads to mass unemployment and mass near starvation.

1911
Unemployment insurance introduced for the first time.

1914-18
Some 200,000 Glaswegians involved in the war effort, either in the armed forces or producing armaments.

1920s
Community of Indian workers develops in Glasgow, largely consisting of labourers and peddlers.

1921
Over half of the 41,000 typists and clerks in Glasgow are women, taking over what were traditionally men's jobs.

1929
The Great Depression, leading to mass unemployment in the 1930s.

1939–45
Glaswegians contribute in great numbers to war effort in the armed forces and in munitions factories.

1944–50
Free secondary and university education, and free health care introduced.

1954
Great improvement in health and safety at work legislation. Nearly half of Glasgow workers involved in manufacturing, a quarter in commerce and finance.

1954–7
5,600 jobs lost in heavy industry in Partick and Govan, 10,000 in Springburn.

1960
Nineteen firemen die in fire in whisky bond in Cheapside Street.

1960s
Asian immigrants take on unskilled work in transport, retail and restaurant sectors.

1962
North British Locomotive Company closes with loss of 5,000 jobs.

1968
Twenty-two upholstery workers die in fire in James Watt Street, unable to escape through barred windows and doors.

1990s
Only one in six Glasgow workers employed in manufacturing, while three out of four work in services. About one in six Glasgow workers is unemployed. Most of these are men and two fifths have been out of work for over a year. Glasgow becomes the third most visited tourist city in Britain.

CHAPTER 7

MADE IN GLASGOW

Before the First World War Glasgow was known as the 'Workshop of the Empire' because of the variety and quantity of goods manufactured in the city and exported all over the world. The roots of this prosperity lie in the eighteenth century, when local merchants made their fortunes trading with the American colonies in tobacco. With the growth of the cotton and later iron industries in the nineteenth century and the rise of shipbuilding and engineering, Glasgow quickly grew into an important centre for industrial manufacturing.

Glasgow had certain advantages which gave it a head start in the development of large-scale manufacturing. Rich supplies of coal and iron ore found around the city provided raw materials for fuelling steam engines and for the manufacture of iron and, later, steel. Industrial achievement can also be ascribed to the business dealings and investments made by a rising group of industrialists linked by shared social and religious values, and often family ties. The city also benefited from the access provided by Britain's large empire to cheap raw materials and overseas markets for export. Crucially, Glasgow's wealth depended on a large labour force. With migration from the Highlands and immigration from Ireland after the 1840s, the city's population rose from 77,000 in 1800 to over one million by 1921, supplying employers with plenty of cheap labour to work in the factories and shipyards as well as the offices and services that supported them.

From the 1870s Britain faced serious competition from America, Germany and, later, Japan. The British industrial economy depended on the heavy industries such as shipbuilding and engineering making local companies vulnerable to slumps in the world economy. Despite an increase in orders during and just after the First and Second World Wars, the picture was one of steady decline in the twentieth century. Locomotive production had already reached its peak production in 1905, and shipbuilding in 1913. Today, only 15 per cent of Glasgow's working population are involved in manufacturing. Most of these jobs are in the engineering, clothing and food and drink industries. Despite attempts to stimulate an increase in manufacturing most people now work in the service industries, including banking, insurance and leisure.

Many objects in the museum collection reflect the ingenuity and diversity of manufacturing in the city over the past 250 years.

Advertisement for Templeton's carpets from Scotland's Industrial Souvenir, *early 1900s.*

TOBACCO

By the 1740s, almost half of all tobacco imported from the American colonies arrived in Glasgow. This was made possible by the Act of Union in 1707 which removed legal barriers against Scottish merchants trading with America. The immense wealth created by the trade was founded on the labour of thousands of black slaves from Africa forced to work on the plantations. The tobacco trade came to an end with the American War of Independence (1775–83), although the city remained a centre of tobacco processing until the 1990s. An offshoot of this industry was the manufacture of clay pipes, many of which were designed to suit the tastes of the countries to which they were exported.

TEXTILES

The demand for cheap cotton cloth caused the dramatic expansion of the cotton industry at the end of the eighteenth century. This increase stimulated the invention of steam-driven spinning and weaving machinery. Raw cotton was first imported from the slave plantations of America and spun into cotton and muslin threads. Many weaving factories specialised in dyeing and printing cloth with fancy patterns and had extensive markets in India and the Far East. After the 1850s, increasing competition from the mills of the north of England forced many firms out of business. However, some companies survived into the 1980s. Glasgow was also famous for carpet-making and examples of those manufactured at Templeton's carpet factory on Glasgow Green can still be seen in many prestigious buildings around the world.

CHEMICALS

This important industry grew out of the need for bleaching powder for use in the textile industry. The St Rollox Works, founded by Charles Tennant in 1798, was at one time one of the largest chemical factories in Europe, and had the tallest chimney in the world. They specialised in the production of bleaching powder, soda, soap products and a range of sulphites and sulphates. Chemical manufacturing continues in the city today, but on a much smaller scale.

IRON AND STEEL

Iron and steel production was the backbone of Glasgow's industrial success. After the invention of the 'hot blast' furnace by J. B. Neilson in 1828, iron production increased using locally mined coal and iron ore. Production was stimulated by a demand for everything from iron plates for building ships down to the rivets which held them together.

Steel production in Glasgow increased substantially after the 1870s. Beardmore's Parkhead Forge contributed to the war effort during both world wars in the production of guns, tanks and munitions. Competition from cheaper foreign steel was a major factor in the decline of the industry, with Beardmore's closing in 1975. The site is now occupied by the Forge Shopping Centre.

Forging a hollow propeller shaft at William Beardmore and Co.'s Parkhead Forge just before the First World War (reproduced courtesy of the Keeper of the Records of Scotland).

The Fairfield Fleet from a painting by A. Burgess, 1907. This painting shows all the warships built or engined at Fairfield's yard in Govan from 1870 to 1907.

ENGINEERING AND MACHINERY

Engineering developed rapidly in the nineteenth century. This was largely as a result of the improvements made to the steam engine by Greenock-born James Watt in the 1760s. Glaswegians manufactured a vast amount of engineering products including coal-cutting and sugar-refining machinery, pumps, cranes, bridges, boilers, electrical equipment and every kind of hand and machine tool. Most of these products were exported all over the world, especially to the Asian and African countries of the British Empire. In the twentieth century the industry declined partly as a result of competition from cheaper foreign products and the failure to develop new technologies.

SHIPBUILDING

From the building of the first steam-powered wooden ships in the early nineteenth century to the steel ships in the 1880s, the Clyde led the world in shipbuilding. Between 1860 and 1913, one third of all British vessels were built on the Clyde. In Glasgow, shipyards at Govan, Partick and Scotstoun built all kinds of ships from yachts and cargo vessels to warships and submarines. Despite government orders during the First and Second World Wars, increasing foreign competition from Germany, Japan and Sweden caused a chronic fall in orders forcing many companies out of business. Attempts by the government to modernise the industry from the 1930s failed and by the 1990s only two shipyards remained in the city.

LOCOMOTIVES

Locomotive production began in the 1830s. Between the 1860s and 1962 over 28,000 locomotives were built of which three quarters were exported. The North British Locomotive Company, based at Springburn, was formed by the amalgamation of the three main companies in 1903 to fight competition from America.

Despite booms during and just after two world wars, overall production fell. NBL could not keep up with new electric and diesel technology leading to the closure of the Springburn works in 1962.

HOUSEHOLD MACHINERY

The presence of a skilled labour force and the opportunities afforded by good transport networks stimulated light engineering production including sewing machines, wringers, mangles and a wide range of domestic machinery. The American Singer Sewing Machine Company was one of many sewing machine factories set up in Glasgow after the 1860s. Singer moved to larger premises in Clydebank in the 1880s where thousands of sewing machines were once made and exported all over the world.

CLOTHING AND SHOES

The clothing industry greatly expanded with the invention of the sewing machine. All kinds of clothes were made in large warehouses and sold to shops at home and overseas. Shoemaking grew out of the leather industry with W. J. Martin in Bridgeton supplying boots and shoes to the troops fighting in the First World War. The Scottish Co-operative Wholesale Society

Shoes made by the Scottish Co-operative Wholesale Society (SCWS), 1930s.

had equal success in shoe manufacturing and was renowned for the quality and value of its wide range of affordable products.

HOUSEHOLD AND LUXURY GOODS

Pottery and silver, glass and pewterware are among the luxury goods made by Glaswegians from the eighteenth century onwards. When the Tobacco Lords imported raw tobacco from America in the eighteenth century, essential and luxury goods were exported to the settlers in the colonies. This stimulated the production of candles, ropes, pottery, glass and pewter in factories around the city. Indeed, one of the principal shareholders in the Delftfield pottery, founded in 1748, was Robert Dinwiddie of Germiston, who later became Governor of Virginia. The most successful pottery in the nineteenth century was J. and M. P. Bell and Co. who enjoyed a huge export market in the Far East where their exotic designs were popular.

FURNITURE

The furniture of Charles Rennie Mackintosh and those who trained at the Glasgow School of Art in the 1890s is now famous all over the world. Their distinctive designs – now known as the 'Glasgow Style' – were popularised by large furnishing stores including Wylie and Lochhead in their range of domestic furniture. Less well-known companies produced shop, hotel and office furniture, and also cheaper furniture for the thousands of new homes built in Glasgow during the nineteenth and twentieth centuries. Decorative stained glass designed and made locally can still be seen in public buildings, churches and houses in Glasgow and beyond.

FOOD AND DRINK

Alcoholic and non-alcoholic drinks are both popular in Glasgow. From 1885, Tennent's Wellpark Brewery, which dates back to the

Plate, J. and M. P. Bell and Co., c. 1890s. One of a collection purchased from an antique shop by a businessman working in Java in the Far East in 1982.

Coal scuttle, 1902, designed by E. A. Taylor (who trained at the Glasgow School of Art) and made by Wylie and Lochhead.

NBL workers with a 2-6-6-0 locomotive, built for South African
Railways in 1920 (reproduced courtesy of Glasgow City Libraries).

Advertisement for 'Camp' coffee. The factory of R. Paterson and Sons expanded in the nineteenth century as coffee became a popular social drink. The Charlotte Street factory closed in the 1980s.

sixteenth century, began exporting lager all over the world, especially to the British Empire. Lager and whisky are still produced in the city today. In the late nineteenth century, non-alcoholic drinks became popular as an alternative to the 'demon drink' with Barr's Irn Bru still a favourite with locals. The Glaswegian sweet tooth stimulated the production of a range of cakes, sweets and biscuits which are still made today in factories and bakeries all over the city.

BOOKS

Printing and publishing were firmly established in the city in the 1740s with the setting up of the Foulis Press by the brothers Robert and Andrew Foulis. Demand for books increased in the nineteenth century as reading became a respectable and affordable pastime for the leisured middle classes, especially women. With large-scale paper production in the city Walter Blackie and William Collins became the largest printers and publishers in Scotland. Children's books, school books and office diaries were sold at home and exported all over the world. By 1928 over 28 million books, especially bibles, were sold by Collins alone. They later printed novels by such authors as Agatha Christie.

CHAPTER 8

MAKING IT IN GLASGOW

The persistence of extremes of poverty in Glasgow has meant that it has not been the city of opportunity many had hoped for when they or their ancestors moved here. For others the city's business and industrial life has provided regular work or opportunities for entrepreneurial adventure. For an exceptionally talented few, the entertainment industry, sport, literature and politics have been escape routes from poverty. Emigration and professional soldiering have also provided means of escape for those who found longed-for greater opportunities than were available in Glasgow. This chapter focuses on famous (and infamous) Glaswegians who made it in Glasgow and those who left the city to seek their fortune elsewhere.

Today Billy Connolly is arguably the most famous Glaswegian, known worldwide. 'The Big Yin', as he was known in Glasgow, became famous using 'old men's patter'. He was born in Partick in 1942 but moved to Drumchapel at the age of four. After working as a delivery boy he was apprenticed as a welder but left the shipyards to become an entertainer. His early material focused on Glasgow and its people. Although he is criticised for being vulgar and giving a bad impression of the city, Glasgow made Billy Connolly popular as surely as Billy Connolly made Glasgow the talk of the chat-show circuit.

Radio Clyde DJ Tiger Tim was starstruck by the glamour of the music business:

I got my City and Guilds certificates, I got two years of them and then I thought I wasn't really learning what

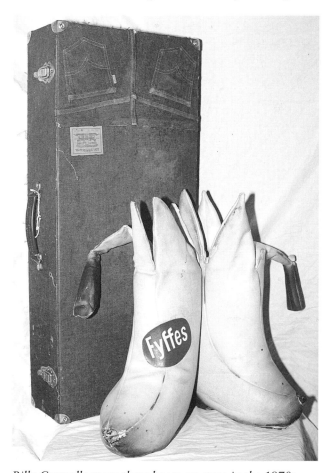

Billy Connolly wore these boots on stage in the 1970s.

Our cameraman, in search of pretty girls, found a blonde and a brunette on the set of Scottish Television's lunchtime show the other morning. Here they are playing hide-and-seek with a camera during a break from rehearsals of " The One O'Clock Gang " at the Theatre Royal in Glasgow. The brunette? Viewers know her well as Dorothy Paul, the Glasgow lass who sings on the show. The blonde? She's a backroom girl you never see, but she's responsible for lots of the settings in various STV programmes. Her name—Helen Rae.

Dorothy Paul (left), c. 1960s.

Liz Lochhead by Alasdair Gray. Poet and playwright, Liz Lochhead (born 1947) performs her poems. Alasdair Gray was commissioned by the People's Palace to produce a series of paintings of people in Glasgow. Today he is better known as a writer.

Ian Pattison, creator of Rab C. Nesbit.

Matt McGinn (1928–77).

I wanted. I was walking round the workshop with a screwdriver talking and singing into it. The guys who were my journeymen had a big cupboard which had a step-in part and they built a stage in it for me. At lunchtimes I would be in this big cupboard and start singing songs and telling jokes.

For successful entertainers, writers and musicians there were substantial financial rewards, as actress and entertainer Dorothy Paul recalls:

I was earning 32/6 a week in the sausage factory, and if I went into variety I would be earning £12 a week, so there was no contest. I ended up in variety and that was it.

Glasgow itself has provided subject matter for local writers and performers:

Glasgow is very interesting for a writer. The absence of a strong literary tradition in Glasgow meant that for a long time it was hard to write about the reality of things. But it's possible now, incidents which you know to be deplorable you store up in your mind and you write about them in ways that you don't quite see at the moment. It's all grist to a writer's mill.

Edwin Morgan, Footsteps and Witnesses, Lesbian and Gay
Life Stories from Scotland

Much of Glasgow writing deals with the realities of life. Sculptor and writer Jimmy Boyle (born 1944) wrote about his experiences of the violence of his life both inside and outside of prison in his book *A Sense of Freedom.* He was sentenced to life imprisonment for murder in 1963. In 1973 he was taken into Barlinnie Special Unit. He was finally released from prison in 1982. His autobiography and the play *The Hard Man,* based on his life and written by Tom McGrath, brought his story to a wider public.

Molly Weir, Meg Henderson, George Rountree, Ralph Glasser and many others have written books about growing up in Glasgow.

Glasgow has influenced a lot of writers: some who were born here; others, like Liz Lochhead and Janice Galloway, who have made Glasgow their home.

Rab C. Nesbit, comic creation of Ian Pattison (whose typewriter is in the collection), inhabits that world of 'deplorable' incidents and is untroubled by boundaries of taste or sensitivity. His Glasgow teems with vice, vermin and domestic violence, and his diet of booze, fags and fat makes the deep-fried Mars bar seem like a healthy snack. It is also a city of contradictions, contrasting the Culture City with its darker side as heart-attack capital of Europe.

Like Ian Pattison's writing, the scripts of performers Dorothy Paul and Francie and Josie express that Glaswegian ability to treat even the most serious subject with humour, and humour is the mainstay of the Glasgow entertainment business. Today's comedians such as Stanley Baxter, Johnny Beattie and Jimmy Logan, and, most recently, stand-up comics such as Jerry Sadowich, carry on the tradition formed in Glasgow's music halls. Tommy Lorne (1890–1935), Dave Willis (1895–1973) and Tommy Morgan (1898–1958) were amongst the first successful Glasgow entertainers.

Songwriters such as Adam McNaughton, who wrote the 'Jeely Piece Song', and Matt McGinn (1928–77), who was born in the Calton and was part of the protest song and folk revival of the 1960s and '70s, wrote of tenement life and the inner city. Pop music provides an opportunity for a few young people to 'make it'. Lulu, one of whose trouser suits is in the collection, was born Marie Lawrie in Dennistoun and first became famous in 1964 with a cover version of the Islay Brother's song 'Shout'. She broke box-office records in 1975 when she played the Pavilion. Today she lives in London and in 1994 sang with Take That. Significant Glasgow bands today include Primal Scream, Teenage Fanclub and Simple Minds, whose platinum disc is in the collection. Other (relatively) local bands like Clydebank-based

The People's Palace Banner
This banner was commissioned from artist Clare Higney in 1989, and shows historic banners from the collection, as well as miniature banners made by members of community groups who visited during her residency in the People's Palace

Watercolour of Glasgow Green dated 1808 showing some of the wooden buildings on the right demolished under Dr James Cleland in the early 1820s

An early shot of the Winter Gardens, 'treasurehouse of the beautiful in shrub and flower' being enjoyed by some local children

ABOVE

Woman shopkeeper 1790

It was unusual for women to own businesses, unless they were widows. In 1789 only two of the seventy-two grocers in Glasgow were women. This woman, possibly Widow Reid of 61 High Street, was obviously well off, which is shown by her gold buckle and earrings

ABOVE RIGHT

Visions of the City gallery at the People's Palace

RIGHT

John Glassford, tobacco merchant, and family, in the Shawfield Mansion Trongate, c1767 by Archibald McLauchlin

This painting shows the wealth of the Glassford family. It is indicative of their social status that they had such a large painting made of themselves. On the left hand side of the painting there is a black servant who has been painted over, possibly when the anti-slavery movement was at its height. There is evidence of black 'servants' being kept in Glasgow and slaves worked on the plantations in Virginia from which Glasgow imported tobacco

'Half a Kitchen' by Thomas McGoran, based on his memories of growing up in a room and kitchen in the 1930s

Glasgow Friendly Association of Cotton Spinners Tray c1825
The Cotton Spinners Friendly Association was one of the strongest unions in Glasgow. Its members controlled the production of cotton, the city's main industry. The tray was probably given as a retirement gift to an office bearer

ABOVE
Rolls Royce workers at the Miners' Strike Rally,
1984

RIGHT
This UCS banner was made in 1981 to celebrate
the ten year anniversary of the Upper Clyde
Shipbuilders work-in and it is now in the
museum collections

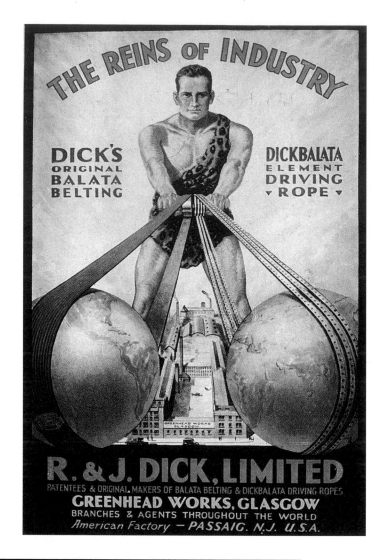

WAVERLEY

THE LAST SEA-GOING
PADDLE STEAMER IN THE WORLD

P.S. Waverley is the most traditional way to view the River Clyde. This map and guide reproduced from the 1950s' timetables allows you to plot your course as we sail 'Doon the Watter'. Whether you join at one of our main ports of call or board at Anderston Quay, we hope you enjoy your sail on the World's Last Sea-Going Paddle Steamer.

LEFT

PS Waverley

BELOW

Boys on PS Waverley *on a day trip doon the watter to Rothesay and Bute, Glasgow Fair, July 1997*

ABOVE

Alex Ferguson, manager of Manchester United Football Club, and players when they won the Premiership 1992/93

LEFT

Billy Connolly by John Byrne.
This portrait of Billy Connolly was painted by John Byrne in 1973 before Connolly became famous. John Byrne first became successful when he pretended to be a primitive artist. He is now a respected artist and writer of plays, most notably the Slab Boys Trilogy *set in a carpet factory. He also wrote television series* Tutti Frutti *and* Your Cheating Heart, *both set in Glasgow*

ABOVE

Portrait of Benny Lynch by Hugh Byers.

RIGHT

Lord Lonsdale Trophy, presented by the British Boxing Board of Control to Benny Lynch on 13 October 1937. He beat Peter Kane at Shawfield Park Stadium in the thirteenth round, for the Flyweight Championship of the world.

Poster announcing the departure of the Bengal Merchant to New Zealand, 1839.

Wet, Wet, Wet have a big following in Glasgow.

Sport, in particular boxing and football, also offered talented Glaswegians the opportunity to break out of a life of poverty. Benny Lynch (1913–46) was Scotland's first world champion boxer. He was born in the Gorbals and was taught to fight by a local priest. He won four world champion title fights with a fifth declared a draw. He died aged 33 from pneumonia after years of alcohol abuse. Although success proved to have its own pressures for Benny Lynch, he was hailed as a hero by Glaswegians, including Jimmy Boyle: 'I didn't have any role models to be honest. There was nobody there. The only ones we had from a distance was Bobby Collins from Celtic or Benny Lynch who was a great boxer.'

The intense popularity of football means that Glasgow has produced great managers and players. When Celtic beat Inter-Milan 2–1 to win the European Cup in 1967 all 11 players who appeared for Celtic in the final came from within a 30-mile radius of Glasgow. When players and managers do become successful they tend to outgrow local clubs and move away. In 1995, along with Alex Ferguson, manager of Manchester United Football Club, there were nine Scottish managers of English football clubs in the Premier division.

For some young, poor and unemployed men from Glasgow, soldiering was a last resort and for many a passport to an early grave. At best it gave them a chance to make a living as well as an opportunity to get out of Glasgow and to travel. In the nineteenth century the army, which maintained Britain's world-wide empire, provided many career opportunities. Commissioned officers from the titled classes joined up for adventure and the chance to prove themselves. Sir Archibald Alison (1826–1907), the son of a baronet and wealthy advocate, was educated at Glasgow University before buying his first commission in 1846. He remained in the army until his death despite having lost an arm when he was sent out to help suppress the Indian Mutiny in 1857. He rose to the rank of General and retired in 1893, having served for ten years on the Indian Council. Two magnificent silver gilt swords presented to him by the City of Glasgow are in the collection, along with a marble portrait bust and trophies from his military conquests in Africa.

Leaving Glasgow either to work away or to emigrate permanently has been an option taken up by many. In the nineteenth century many people who could afford to left Glasgow hoping to find a better life in the new worlds of America, New Zealand and Australia, people such as those Lucian Laing, born in the 1920s, met:

I was over in Baltimore and I had to go into dry dock. A guy came on board and told me to go over to see his old mate from Glasgow. So I went over and introduced myself and it turned out he had served his time in Fairfield shipyards but then he went over to the States.

Others, like self-made millionaire Thomas Lipton (1850–1931), who was the son of Irish immigrants, came to Glasgow from elsewhere. John Wheatley (1869–1930), also the son of Irish Catholic immigrants, rose from poverty to become a successful businessman and politician, introducing a Housing Act in the first ever Labour Government of 1924. The Wheatley Act gave subsidies to local authorities to help them build houses and to help pay rents out of local taxes.

Manager of Manchester United Football Club, Alex Ferguson, believes that the recipe for success in any field is hard work:

> You have to be a worker. You have to work. That is as good a recipe for success as you will get anywhere. Talent doesn't earn a penny. Work earns the money and that is my secret.

HIM! A KENT HIS FAITHER!

Successful people such as Alex Ferguson and Billy Connolly can give rise to admiration, inspiration and envy among Glaswegians. Glasgow people often have a love-hate relationship with people who leave the city. Comedian Andy Cameron, speaking on BBC Radio Scotland's *The People's Patter* in December 1996, believes that, 'Billy Connolly finds it [Glasgow] difficult 'cos he's gone away. He's done the Hollywood bit . . . and I'm

'Patter Merchant', Andy Cameron (photograph courtesy of Peter de Rance, Chalmers Wood Limited).

delighted for him. I think that's marvellous. But the punters! What are ye doing here. Away and have tea with the Queen, ya!'

Although fame and fortune will always be the reward for the very few, Glasgow has provided different opportunities at different times. Ian Pattison urges people to grasp those opportunities:

> I think the message is, if I can do it then anyone can do it. I've got my fat arse on a script editing chair at the BBC. I used to cycle past the BBC when I was 15 delivering telegrams and I used to think you had to go to university for 98 years and have an income of £3 million pounds to get in the front door.

Loading on the Clyde for Africa, 1950s.

CHAPTER 9

GLASGOW'S RIVER

Glasgow made the Clyde and the Clyde made Glasgow

When the town of Glasgow was founded it had little use for the marshy meandering river full of sandbanks on its doorstep, other than as a source of salmon. When the Broomielaw quay was built in 1662 small ships began to come into Glasgow, but it was not until the Cheshire engineer John Goldborne was engaged in 1768 that any real progress was made in deepening the Clyde. His idea was to 'assist nature' by building a series of jetties which would make the river narrower and faster, scouring the bed of the river. With the additional assistance of primitive mud ploughs, the depth of the river was doubled to around five feet, and in 1780 the first seagoing ship berthed at Glasgow.

This was to be the first of many, and as trade grew so did industry. The first major industries in Glasgow were cotton spinning and mining but engineering works soon grew up to supply them with machinery. These engineering firms in turn supplied the engines for the first steamships. The introduction of the steamship in 1812 provided an even greater impetus for further development of the river as ships could now steam up the river without waiting for wind or tide. Steam power also provided the

means to deepen the river further.

The first shipyard in Glasgow was at the mouth of the Kelvin, but in 1840 Robert Napier, the 'father of the Clyde shipbuilding', opened a shipyard at Govan. Many more shipyards followed and under Napier's influence the Clyde gained a worldwide reputation for the quality of its ships, and 'Clyde-built' became one of the greatest accolades a ship could have. Iron and steel ships were Glasgow's speciality, and the racket of thousands of riveters battering the ships together could be heard across the city; the 'hammer's ding-dong' became The Song of the Clyde.

Other industries also grew on the banks of the Clyde, such as chemical works and iron foundries, which used the river as a convenient way of disposing of waste products. What was once a peaceful salmon river became a vile and putrid sewer as this industrial effluent mixed with the untreated human waste of the city's ever growing population.

Management of the Clyde through various bodies, such as the River Improvement Trust (1809), was in the hands of the town council. External pressure led, in 1840, to the inclusion of representatives of the Trades House, the Merchants' House and the neighbouring boroughs of Gorbals, Calton and Anderston. This was reconstituted in 1858 as the Clyde

Navigation Trust. The work of these bodies meant that the largest ships afloat could make their way up to Glasgow, and to cater for the growing demand new quays and docks were built, each with its own special purpose. The Broomielaw was for passenger traffic down the Clyde coast, Yorkhill for transatlantic liners and Queen's Dock for the Far East liners and general cargo ships. Coal was exported from Prince's Dock, while cattle arrived at Merkland's Lairage and grain at Meadowside. At its peak the port of Glasgow had over ten miles of quay frontage and handled over ten million tons of cargo a year.

As the quays developed a dockland community grew up that worked and lived in the shadow of the cranes. On the streets surrounding the docks were countless seedy pubs and brothels where the dockers and shipyard workers mingled with the sailors from across the seas. The work was tough and accidents common, but there was a great humour among the men. There is one instance of a docker, on being told by his gaffer to capture an escaped bull, complaining: 'I'm a stevedore no' a bloody toreador!'

The docks held a fascination for young and old alike. George Rountree remembers being taken to the docks as a child by his Granda' in the 1930s:

Docks always seemed to be busy and quays a hive of activity then. With ships being unloaded and reloaded, with horse-drawn, motorised and steam-powered vehicles, and hand barrows as well, constantly coming and going, and crowds of dockers stacking the loads on vehicles as they came off the boats.

George Rountree, A Govan Childhood:
the 1930s (Edinburgh, 1993)

With the river and docks so well developed the city was effectively cut in half. The Clyde Navigation Trust operated a series of passenger and vehicle ferries that criss-crossed the river at various points, with the busiest crossing between Govan and Partick. The famous Clutha ferries also ran up and down the river.

However, the story of the Clyde is not all about trade and industry. The first steamships were used to carry passengers on pleasure trips. As the resorts of Rothesay, Largs and Millport developed demand for a trip 'doon the watter' became phenomenal and the Clyde pleasure steamer fleet grew to impressive proportions. The annual 'fair fortnight' saw thousands of workers rushing to flee the city. One fair Saturday morning in 1883 more than 15,000 people were carried down the river in a fleet of over twenty steamers. Eventually this steamer

traffic dwindled as the railways provided a quicker route to the coast and avoided the filth of the upper river.

Further upstream Glasgow Green provided the more sedate pleasure of riverside walks and the Glasgow citizens stoutly defended their parkland against the attentions of the dock engineers. Swimming and boating also became popular pastimes and the regattas provided one of the city's great spectator sports before the days of football. These activities became infinitely more pleasurable after the opening of Dalmarnock sewage works in 1894. Walter Freer, in *My Life and Memories* (Glasgow, 1929) remembered what it was like to swim before then:

> It is a wonder we did not all of us die of disease, for the water was filthy. The wash from the print works coloured the water brown, and looking back, I can almost believe that the very water was poisoned.

A spell in the Clyde was not always a pleasant experience and in 1790 the Glasgow Humane Society was founded, with its headquarters on Glasgow Green, to rescue those bodies that fell into the Clyde, whether by accident or design.

The first signs of Glasgow's industrial decline came in the great depression of the 1920s and '30s when work in the shipyards came to a halt and traffic on the river fell sharply. However, it was not until after the Second World War that the real decline began. Foreign yards with more enlightened managers and less conservative workers took work from the increasingly outdated Clyde shipyards. Cheap air travel destroyed Glasgow's passenger shipping trade, and the increasing size of ships and new cargo handling methods made Glasgow's docks redundant virtually overnight. The speed and scale of the decline were remarkable. No one standing in the bustling docks in 1960 could have foreseen that in twenty years the Clyde would be empty of ships, the docks infilled and only two shipyards left working on the river.

In the 1980s Glasgow set about regenerating its derelict dockland. Luxury housing was built in some of the old warehouses, the Scottish Exhibition and Conference Centre was built on the site of Queen's Dock, and in 1988 the Garden Festival was built on Prince's Dock. However, the regeneration has not been a total success. Successive attempts to create a maritime heritage centre in the old Govan dry-docks have so far come to nothing, but a Millenium funded Science Park is planned for the Garden Festival Site.

For many years the 'sludgie boats' were about the only ships sailing up and down the Clyde, but even these stopped in 1998 after the introduction of new regulations on dumping at sea. Clydeport, the successor of the Clyde Navigation Trust, now makes its money from property development rather than harbour dues, but the Finnieston crane will always stand as a memorial to the proud days of industry. The *Waverley* now sails on as the only ship to keep company with the salmon that have returned to the Clyde.

Old Glasgow Bridge 1816/17, by John Knox.

The cenotaph in George Square commemorates all those who died in the First and Second World Wars. It was unveiled by Earl Haig in May 1924.

CHAPTER 10

A TALE FROM THE TRENCHES (1914-18)

Live clean or go out quick.
Lads, you're wanted. Come and die.

Ewart Alan Mackintosh, 'Recruiting', 1917

When Britain declared war on Germany on 4 August 1914, most people believed that the war would be over by Christmas. It was felt that Germany would be quickly defeated by the united forces of Britain, France and Russia. The reality of what followed could not have been more different. Between 1914 and 1918 over half a million Scots enlisted or were conscripted to fight in the war and over 125,000 were killed in some of the bloodiest battles ever fought in modern history. From the war come stories of remarkable heroism, self-sacrifice and personal tragedy which are remembered year after year on Remembrance Sunday at war memorials up and down the country.

The declaration of war on Germany took many people by surprise. The Secretary of State for War, Lord Kitchener, immediately launched a nationwide appeal for volunteers to fight 'for King and Country'. In the first ten weeks of war nearly 30,000 men enlisted in Glasgow alone. In January 1916, as the war continued, conscription was introduced and thousands more were called up. Not everyone was enthusiastic about Britain's involvement in the war. The Glasgow socialist John Maclean (1879–1923) was among a vociferous group of conscientious objectors who publicly denounced it as a pointless capitalist war.

One young man who volunteered only weeks

after war was declared was James Riley, a twenty-five-year-old driller who lived in Armour Street, off the Gallowgate. He enlisted with the Cameronians (Scottish Rifles), a regiment with strong Glasgow ties, and was assigned to the

Private James Riley.

The shaving mirror and German drill book which saved Private Riley's life.

In the collection are letters and cards exchanged between Private Riley and his wife Jeannie offering a unique insight into life in wartime Glasgow. She talks about the family, the impact of the war on their lives and tells him the latest family gossip:

I hope you were not angry at me only sending the 2/- postal order as I had 14/- for rent and things are getting so dear here.

Due to the huge numbers of men who had enlisted or were conscripted, Jeannie, along with thousands of other women, worked in shipyards and factories producing ships, munitions and uniforms. In her letters she describes her work in the engineering section of Yarrows shipyard in Scotstoun in the west of the city. For thousands of women like Jeannie this was their first experience of working in heavy industry. From a letter dated 23 March 1916 it is clear she took a great pride in her work and highlights the anxiety of many male workers at the women's presence in the shipyard:

Machine Gun Corps. A unique collection of objects in the museum tells the amazing story of how he narrowly escaped death when shot by a German soldier.

Riley had been in the firing line for nine months when he was hit by a German explosive bullet above the heart. In his tunic pocket he carried a small electroplated shaving mirror and a German soldier's drill book. The bullet passed through the book but was prevented from entering his chest by the shaving mirror, which absorbed most of the impact. Private Riley had probably picked up the drill book from the battlefield as a souvenir of the war; they were given to all German soldiers by the Kaiser and contained practical information and prayers. This amazing story featured in a newspaper article, which he also kept. Private Riley recovered at Woodside Hospital in Glasgow before returning to the trenches.

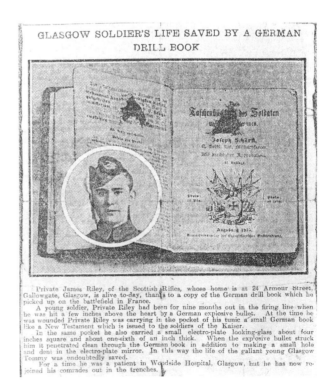

GLASGOW SOLDIER'S LIFE SAVED BY A GERMAN DRILL BOOK

Private James Riley, of the Scottish Rifles, whose home is at 24 Armour Street, Gallowgate, Glasgow, is alive to-day, thanks to a copy of the German drill book which he picked up on the battlefield in France.

A young soldier, Private Riley had been for nine months out in the firing line when he was hit a few inches above the heart by a German explosive bullet. At the time he was wounded Private Riley was carrying in the pocket of his tunic a small German book like a New Testament which is issued to the soldiers of the Kaiser.

In the same pocket he also carried a small electro-plate looking-glass about four inches square and about one-sixth of an inch thick. When the explosive bullet struck him it penetrated clean through the German book in addition to making a small hole and dent in the electro-plate mirror. In this way the life of the gallant young Glasgow Tommy was undoubtedly saved.

For a time he was a patient in Woodside Hospital, Glasgow, but he has now rejoined his comrades out in the trenches.

Newspaper article on Riley's lucky escape.

Dear Jamie, I am still sticking in at my work. I will be an engineer before long! There are 25 more women coming in on Monday . . . and we were told that the amount of work we do in three weeks would have taken the men three years and Jamie the men are quite mad at us.

This taste of tough industrial work was liberating for thousands of women, despite the dangerous conditions, and many, including Jeannie, showed no intention of giving it up when the men returned from the war:

I am up at half past four every morning, so I will have you up at the same time when you come back if God spares you.

A woman I work with – her name is Murphy – she lives in the Gallowgate near us . . . she lost her finger in a machine in the work, but she's a tough one. Once she came back from the Western Infirmary, she carried on like nothing had happened.

Embroidered card sent by James Riley to his wife Jeannie when on active service.

In Glasgow families like the Rileys struggled to continue living as normally as possible. To ease the hardships many were facing, a National Relief Fund headed by the Prince of Wales was set up to which Glaswegians gave nearly £240,000 within six months. Life became even more difficult in 1918 when food rationing was introduced as the German U-boats increasingly

The engineering section, Yarrows shipyard. Jeannie is standing between two other women in the centre of the photograph.

A Rent Strike demonstration, Govan, 1915 (from The Bulletin).

cut off supplies to the British ports. Posters encouraging people to make the most of their rations were posted up throughout the city.

Private landlords took advantage of the demand for workers' housing and put up rents, causing misery to thousands of families. In the summer of 1915, women from Govan, Partick, Oatlands, Dennistoun, Ibrox, Bellahouston and Parkhead demonstrated against evictions and encouraged people to stop paying their rent. There were angry scenes when factors tried to evict the families of soldiers who were fighting in the war. Wide support for the rent strikes came from across the city including the Glasgow Labour Party Housing Committee, trade unions and even some employers. When munitions workers came out in strike in support, the government launched an inquiry. With the direct involvement of Lloyd George, then Minister of Munitions, the government passed the Rent Restrictions Act in November 1915, freezing rents at the same rate they had been in 1914. They could not risk strikes by workers whose contribution to the war effort in the factories and shipyards was vital for Britain to win the war.

When the armistice was signed on 11 November 1918 there was great rejoicing. However, as the soldiers gradually returned to their families, the human cost of victory became clear. Over 20 million people, including 20,000 Glaswegians, had been killed and many more injured. Private Riley returned to his family and treasured the shaving mirror and drill book for the rest of his life. Unlike thousands of his comrades, he lived to tell the tale.

CHAPTER 11

THE HOME FRONT (1939-45)

One of my earliest memories is sitting on my dad's shoulders in a street in Springburn at night looking at the bombing. We stayed three stairs up and we had an uninterrupted view of Clydebank. I'll never forget the red glow and the noise of the bombing.

Jim Provan's childhood memory highlights one of the major differences between the First and Second World Wars. For the first time Glasgow suffered heavy bombing. The presence of shipyards and heavy engineering factories whose output of ships, tanks and munitions was an important part of the war effort, meant the city was a target for aerial attack. This chapter looks at how the war years affected Glaswegians who, despite the rationing and the air raids, struggled to continue life as normal.

The outbreak of war in Europe was the culmination of years of tension and suspicion as Germany, under the control of the Nazis and leadership of Adolf Hitler, began increasing its armed forces and annexing territory. Hitler's intention was the creation of a large empire and to this end he invaded Austria (March 1938) and the German-speaking areas of Czechoslovakia (September 1938). In March 1939 he annexed the whole of the country, with the acquiescence of Britain and France. However, when Hitler invaded Poland (September 1939), Britain and France decided he had to be stopped. The war clouds finally burst with the declaration of war on Germany on 3 September 1939. In 1941, when war broke out in the Pacific and the Far East, the conflict in Europe was transformed into a world war.

As a result of the growing German threat,

Britain began preparations for war from 1935. The government ordered every local authority to set up an Air Raids Precautions (ARP) Committee to prepare everyone for the threat of aerial bombing. A chief air raid warden was appointed in Glasgow in 1937 and voluntary air raid wardens, decontamination squads and police, fire and medical services were trained how to cope with emergencies, especially gas attacks. As a precaution, everyone was issued with gas masks, including small babies, as Mary McPhater recalls:

These information leaflets were distributed to prepare the population for war.

*'Air Raid Warning'. One of a collection of powerful wartime etchings by Ian Fleming, who worked as a
Police Reserve Sergeant at Maryhill Police Station.*

I had one of these gas mask things for my baby and
no way could I use it. I had to send it back because
I had two other wee ones under three that I had
to put a gas mask on. I couldn't even put one on
myself. I hadn't even the patience!

The public were kept informed by the ARP
through leaflets and exhibitions. Drills were
organised to demonstrate what to do in the event
of an air raid.

By the time war broke out, 381 fully trained
wardens were in place and ready for action. They
had the key role of contacting the emergency
services in the event of an air raid and reporting
any damage. Each was given responsibility for a
specific ward or area of the city, similar to a
police beat, and was trained to make sure all the
necessary guidelines were followed during an
attack, as May Hutton recalls:

You hadn't to show a light, the windows were
taped so that the glass didn't come in. You also had
curtains and blankets – anything that would stop
light from showing. If there was a wee chink of
light, the air raid warden would blow his whistle.

Thousands of shelters were set up all over the
city, using backcourts, tenement basements,
tunnels and even underneath railway arches.
One of the most popular for people with
gardens was the Anderson shelter, named after
Sir John Anderson, a cabinet minister with
special responsibilities for air raid precautions.
This shelter, made of corrugated steel sheets,
was sunk into the ground to a depth of a metre
and partly covered with earth or sandbags to
withstand near bomb blasts. Lily Miller
remembers using this type of shelter:

'Air Raid Shelter' from an etching by Ian Fleming.

I always remember a man telling us not to lean forward in the shelter as there wasn't much earth on it. That was the night of the Clydebank blitz and the bombing. I was only 15 at the time. We sat in there from nine at night until six in the morning.

Frequent drills trained people to recognise the sound of the air raid warning and the 'All Clear' signal when it was safe to leave.

A further preparation for war was the planned evacuation of thousands of children from the city to the safety of the countryside to avoid the worst effects of the bombing. Many children who had never been outside the city thought this was a great adventure; others were upset at leaving their families behind and living with complete strangers. Evacuation was voluntary and some mothers accompanied their children. The government issued special guidelines instructing parents to pack only the essentials for their children in one small suitcase. However, many families could not even afford the minimum that was recommended, as Ruby Riddell recalls:

I was evacuated to Aberfeldy in Perthshire. We didn't have a suitcase. I took a wee brown poke with a jersey and a pair of knickers in it.

All the children had labels with their names pinned on their coats so they would be recognised when they got to their destination. As the expected bombing of Glasgow and Clydebank did not happen straight away, most children returned to their families over the winter of 1939. However, with the heavy bombing in March 1941, many more were re-evacuated.

Evacuees leaving Glasgow wearing identity labels, May 1941 (photograph courtesy of the Herald and Evening Times).

Clearing up after the Scotstoun blitz, 1940 (photograph courtesy of the Herald and Evening Times).

The first air raid came in July 1940 with a daylight attack on the city. Some of the worst bombing took place on the nights of 13/14 March 1941 and many, including George Telfer, were caught by surprise at the scale of the raid:

We didn't have a shelter at that time so we went down the stair to the first landing and sat in an old woman's lobby. She was really worried and saying, 'Oh here they're coming.' We were saying to her that it was only a strong wind and she said, 'It must be some wind – it's blowing the windows in!'

The nearby town of Clydebank was devastated and damage to the city itself was spread over a large area in the west and north-west of the city including Maryhill, Govan, Partick, Scotstoun, Knightswood and Yoker. In all 1,083 people were killed in Glasgow and Clydebank on those terrifying nights, with thousands more injured. Lily Miller vividly recalls the night's events:

It was a bright, bright moonlit night. I remember when we came out the shelter, all the bricks were lying and my mother was crying and saying, 'That's our house away.'

One place particularly badly affected centred on the Kilmun Street area of Maryhill where whole families were killed in the blast, including seven children.

As Britain depended to a large extent on overseas countries for food supplies, and as

Group of Glasgow children celebrating VE day, Partick, 1945.

rationed by weight. Mary McPhater remembers the effects of rationing:

> If you had children, it wasn't too bad. Of course you did without to give to your children, but if you lived alone or were a couple, it was pretty bad.

As the war raged on, rationing became more severe. Everyone was encouraged to make best use of what they had as razor blades, stockings and even make-up were in short supply. Sweets, petrol, clothing and soap were eventually rationed, and fuel shortages meant frequent power cuts.

With the advance of the Allied Forces through Europe and the eventual surrender of Germany on 8 May 1945, the war in Europe finally came to an end. However, conflict in the Far East and Pacific did not end until 15 August with the surrender of Japan. As soon as the end of the war in Europe was announced, Glaswegians began celebrating. Streets and buildings were decorated with flags and bunting and many areas organised their own street parties to celebrate VE day. It took many years to recover from the effects of the war. Building new houses had been suspended and thousands of already crumbling tenements had to be demolished, so that the housing shortage was worse than ever. In the 1950s this led to the creation of massive housing schemes on the outskirts of the city. The industrial boom during and just after the war masked the long-term decline of Glasgow's industries. Most people were taken by surprise when they collapsed in the 1960s.

ships increasingly came under attack, rationing was introduced. Everyone was given a ration book. Families had to register with a particular butcher and grocer who had enough rations each week for the people on their lists. Food was

CHAPTER 12

THE BEVVY

Alcoholic drink is an important aspect of Glaswegian culture, most recently 'glamorised' on television by the notorious character of Rab C. Nesbit. Over 90 per cent of Scots drink alcohol. Many drink to relax with friends, and when taken in moderation alcohol can be part of a healthy lifestyle. Alcohol is, however, a powerful addictive drug and constant heavy drinking can damage people's health and cause problems at home and at work. Since the early nineteenth century, alcohol abuse has been highlighted as a major problem for Glasgow. Over the years attempts have been made by voluntary organisations and the city authorities to encourage people to reduce their level of drinking or to abstain from alcohol altogether.

In eighteenth-century Glasgow, heavy drinking bouts were considered a respectable pastime by the wealthy middle and upper classes. Much of this centred on private drinking clubs where men drank till they literally fell to the floor. The Saracen Head Inn punch bowl is a relic from these times. Broken and repaired on many occasions, it bears testimony to heavy group drinking sessions. The bowl was made in the 1760s by the Delftfield Pottery Company in Glasgow which exported many of their products to the American colonies. It was last used at a special dinner of the Glasgow Archaeological Society in 1860.

The Drover, Gallowgate, early 1990s (the Glasgow Photo Archive, Cranhill Arts).

Early in the nineteenth-century opinions about drinking began to change. As the population of the city exploded dramatically, drinking became a cheap way of coping with the misery of poverty. Alcoholism was rife and more and more people, especially among the middle classes, increasingly saw alcohol abuse and its effects as a major problem and a threat to moral and social order. Alcohol abuse by irresponsible individuals who required discipline and/or religious guidance was a convenient explanation for the obvious poverty and ill health visited upon a large proportion of the population by poor wages, unreliable work and appalling housing conditions.

LEFT
Saracen Head Inn punch bowl, 1760s.

BELOW
Barrow used by Govan police to carry drunks off to jail, late nineteenth century.

The temperance movement, which aimed at curbing alcohol abuse, was brought to the city by John Dunlop (1789–1868) in the late 1820s, and he, along with the support of the printer William Collins (1789–1853), set about educating people about the dangers of drinking. Some of the earliest support came from religious organisations such as the Glasgow City Mission, founded in 1826. They had first-hand experience of the effects of alcohol on the poor and destitute, as seen in this extract from a report of 1854:

Out of the twelve families I visited today, I do not think that more than one woman is living at peace with her husband. The men are all drunkards and abuse their poor wives when under the influence of strong drink.

From the 1830s, branches of temperance societies sprang up all over Glasgow. Thousands of people 'took the pledge', promising either to abstain from all forms of alcoholic drinks or in some instances from spirits only. Temperance fever became part of the evangelical revival of the nineteenth century. Organisations such as the Glasgow United Evangelical Association, based at the former Tent Hall near the Saltmarket, even provided entertainment in the form of lantern slide shows as an alternative to the Saturday night 'demon drink' ritual. One of these slides depicts a man before and after he was 'saved' and also illustrates the moral and financial benefits of adopting an alcohol-free lifestyle.

The temperance movement was very influential in Glasgow. In 1853 under the Licensing (Scotland) Act the opening hours of public houses were limited to 11 p.m. and all pubs were closed on Sunday. In 1890, the town council agreed that no more licences would be granted to sell alcohol on corporation property. The movement was also supported at the highest level. Many lord provosts, councillors

1910.

1912.

'Before and after' from a Tent Hall lantern slide.

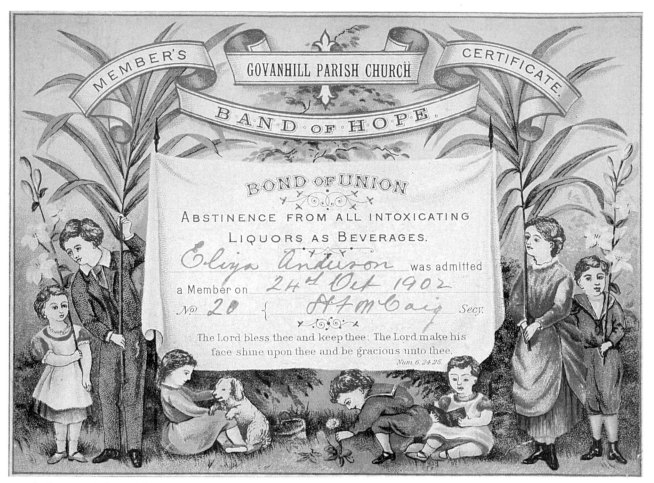

Band of Hope pledge card, 1902.

and politicians, including the socialists Keir Hardie (1856–1915) and John Maclean (1879–1923), were lifelong supporters of temperance causes. After the Temperance (Scotland) Act of 1913, whole areas of the city and surrounding districts voted to limit the number of public houses in their district and refused new applications for licences. Many areas such as Pollokshields, Cathcart and the new housing schemes such as Castlemilk had very few pubs well into the 1970s.

Today, Glasgow has one of the highest rates of heart disease in Europe and alcohol abuse, along with smoking and poor diet, is seen as a major cause. The campaign against alcohol has been taken up by health authorities and alcohol advisory councils who actively encourage everyone, through education, to adopt a healthier lifestyle and limit the amount of alcohol consumed. Alcohol is now banned at football matches, and a controversial bye-law forbidding drinking in public places was introduced by the council in 1996.

Concern about under-age drinking and the effects of alcohol abuse on children led to the formation of the Scottish Band of Hope Union in Glasgow in 1871. One of its earliest supporters was William Quarrier, who later founded children's orphanages in Glasgow and Bridge of Weir where children – many of them victims of abuse by alcoholic parents – were cared for. The Band of Hope continues today in their campaign against drugs as well as alcohol abuse.

CHAPTER 13

CRIME AND PUNISHMENT

Glasgow's regeneration, from the opening of the Burrell Collection in 1983 to its year as European City of Culture in 1990, may have gone a long way to changing its reputation as a den of drunkenness, hard men, street gangs, violence and vice, vividly portrayed in McArthur and Long's 1935 novel *No Mean City*. Even today the chequered and/or imagined history of Glasgow as a capital of crime remains a part of the media view of the city, though it is unlikely that crime was or is worse there than in any other large British city. So pervasive is the hard man image that visitors to Glasgow have to be reminded that the hit film *Trainspotting* is actually set in Edinburgh. Ironically, it is possible that much of Glasgow's image as a crime-ridden city came from the campaigns mounted by nineteenth-century middle-class local government politicians and officials, religious and social reformers. Their efforts to maintain order in the rapidly growing city, and especially to limit the curse of excessive drinking, drew attention to its evils.

BANISHMENT

Although prison is today the commonest punishment for a range of crimes, from non-payment of fines to murder, in the eighteenth and nineteenth centuries banishment was an option. Glaswegians who broke the law could be transported to America (until 1776) or Australia (until 1852). Over this period 1,500 Scottish women convicts were sent to New South Wales at the request of the Australian authorities in order to increase the female population. Women were allowed to take young children with them. From around 1850 onwards prison sentences began to be given as this cost the state less than transportation, and settlers in the New World were complaining about the numbers of convicts.

'YE'LL DEE FACIN' THE MONUMENT'

In the late eighteenth century there were over 200 crimes which carried the death penalty, and most of these were forms of theft. During the nineteenth century the reform movement gradually reduced the number of crimes which were punishable by death in favour of transportation. For many years executions were carried out in public because the authorities thought that people would be deterred from committing the same crime. Hanging was the usual method, beheading being reserved for the aristocracy. Early execution sites were: Howgate Head (1765–81) where seven hangings were carried out; Castle Yard; High Street

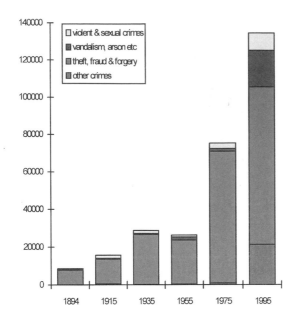

Chart showing reported crimes 1894–1995. Note the
increase in the number of violent and sexual crimes being
reported. This may not mean that they did not happen in
earlier years.

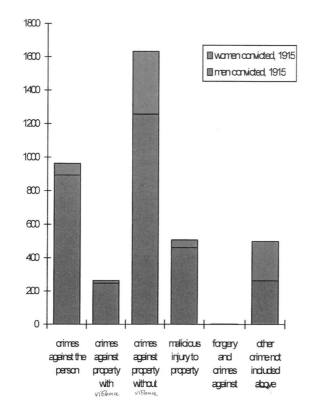

Bar chart showing the numbers of men and women
convicted for a range of crimes, 1915.

(1784–1778) where 12 people were hanged, two
of whom were women; and Glasgow Cross
1788–1813 where there were a total of 22
hangings including one woman. In 1814 the
execution site moved to Jail Square at Glasgow
Green, outside the newly built judiciary
buildings. In total, 67 men and four women were
to 'dee facin' the Monument', a saying alluding
to Nelson's Monument, the last sight the
prisoner saw.

Public hangings were a festive occasion and
whole families waited for hours to get a good
view. Even small children were allowed to
watch. Food and drink were sold from street
stalls and entertainers helped to pass the time.
The last person to be hanged on the Green was
poisoner Dr Pritchard in 1865, and 80,000
people came to see him die. From then until the
abolition of hanging in 1960 executions were
carried out in private with only a few witnesses.
From 1865 to 1928 hangings took place in
Duke Street prison. The bell now on display in
the People's Palace was rung to announce the
execution and served as a warning to all who
heard it, as Jenny Lyle, born in the 1910s,
remembers:

Many notorious prisoners were enclosed there.
Some were hanged there in the prison grounds.
They were always hanged at eight o'clock in the
morning and the black flag went up and the bell
tolled when they were dead.

Barlinnie became the execution site for
Glasgow in 1928, though the first execution did
not take place there until 1946, when John Lyon
was hanged for the murder of John Brady. The
executioner was Albert Pierrepoint. Executed
prisoners were buried within the grounds of the
prison, their bodies covered with quicklime.
Anthony Miller, hanged on 22 December 1960,
was the last person to be executed in Glasgow.
He was also, at 19, the youngest person to be
executed in Scotland in the twentieth century.
The execution chamber, which was equipped to
hang three people at once, was demolished in

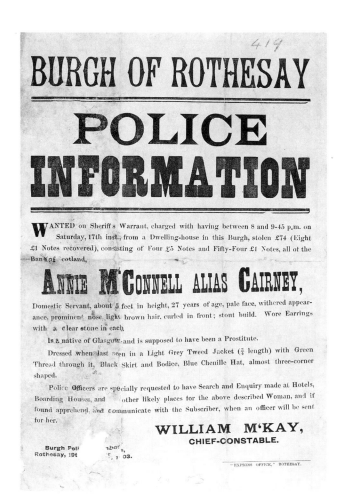

Wanted poster. Posters relating to crime were the most common printed material in the nineteenth century. More people would have seen these than newspapers.

1996, with internal fittings being preserved by the National Museums of Scotland.

HELL MEND YE

In the eighteenth century the Tolbooth was the main place for holding prisoners in Glasgow, who were mostly vagrants. As the population of Glasgow grew so did the prison population and more prison space was needed. A new jail at the Saltmarket, which opened in 1814, was soon outgrown and Duke Street prison was built. From 1825 Duke Street, built on the site of an earlier correction house, became the main prison in Glasgow. It was a mixed prison until Barlinnie opened in 1882 when it became a women's prison. It closed in 1955. Barlinnie is now the only prison within the city boundary. Cornton Vale, Stirlingshire, is the nearest women's prison. Though Duke Street was demolished in 1958, this children's rhyme – 'Duke Street Gaol' – shows that it remains part of Glasgow folklore:

> There is a happy land
> doon in Duke Street Gaol
> Where a' the prisoners stand
> hanging on a nail
> Ham and eggs they'll never see
> bread and butter fur their tea
> Live their lives in misery
> God save the Queen

Class and gender influenced the type and number of crimes and also the way in which prisoners were treated. The vast majority of prisoners in Barlinnie have been and are working-class men between 18 and 24. Many, like Dave (born 1963), were imprisoned for violence and alcohol- and drug-related crimes.

The mortuary slab in the lower room of the death chamber, Barlinnie prison (photograph courtesy of Tom O'Brien).

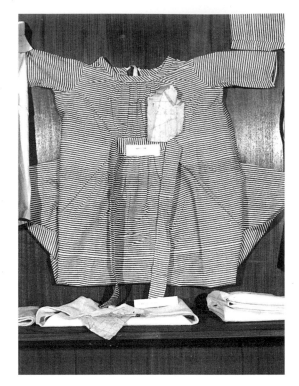

FROM TOP LEFT (clockwise)

Bell from Duke Street prison which was rung to announce the death of executed prisoners; Clothes made for babies born in prison, c. 1920; Prisoners in Barlinnie prison, 1995; This scroll to his parents was made by a young man in Barlinnie in 1995. He had just been given a ten-year sentence.

He was first sent to Barlinnie in 1985 for carrying an offensive weapon with intent to use:

> I was 21, out one night with my pal and I went out with a hatchet. I went towards the crowd and I just felt a bang on the back of my head and I was doon on the deck and the thing taken off me. So I got the jail. I do have a drink when I am out and if someone says something to me I'm a nippy-sweetie. I admit that.

Women commit fewer crimes than men, and far fewer violent crimes; most go to prison for unpaid fines, prostitution and shoplifting. Until the eighteenth century few women were imprisoned in Glasgow. After 1800 the numbers of women prisoners increased, but some women who broke the law were treated for mental illness and could be sent to asylums. Today only one in 30 prisoners is female. Up until the twentieth century women could keep small children with them in prison. Children wore clothes made from the same material as the prison uniforms. Today only babies up to 12 months are kept in prison. It is this separation from children which is the most painful aspect of prison life for many women:

> I think the minute you walk in that door you are reminded that because of you your weans are away. Because of you, you have just lost your hoose. Because of you your weans are going to grow up with a complex. Women are told that.
>
> *Karen (born 1961), who spent 23 months and two weeks in Cornton Vale in the 1970s*

PRISON CULTURE

In 1852 hard labour was introduced as it was thought that prison life was too easy. This meant prisoners had to perform repetitive and often pointless tasks. Common forms of hard labour were picking oakum (separating tarred rope) or turning crank wheels. Today all prisoners are required to work. Women tend to do domestic work such as cooking and sewing.

Overcrowding and a violent culture in prisons compound the loss of liberty and create a separate way of life to which people are forced to adjust. K, who was imprisoned in Cornton Vale, reflected:

> Prison takes people who are already damaged in some way or another and by the time they have went through the system, even if it is just one night in a police station, they are further damaged. If you keep proceeding through that system you will eventually become a destroyed, brutalised human being. It is no wonder that people come out of jail and have no conscience – no sense of right and wrong. They are brutalised.

Passing the time in prison can be extremely difficult and prisoners can find a degree of release in creative activity. In Barlinnie today this is encouraged, but often artworks are made secretly using only the materials which can be found in prison. The decorations on boxes made from cigarette tins using matchsticks and egg-shells remind prisoners of the things that they miss from life outside – girlfriends and football teams. One of the most evocative, and in some ways puzzling, objects in the museum collection is a brush, on which Andrew Hardie carved the Glasgow Coat of Arms while in prison for his part in the 1820 Rising, for which he was eventually executed.

VICTIMS OF CRIME

Most victims of crime are from the same community as the criminals, often with the strong preying on the vulnerable. Thus, while most reported violent crime is committed by young men against other young men, words like 'mugging', 'petty theft' and 'burglary' often conceal major traumas for the victims, especially the loss of a sense of being safe in one's own home or street. Even witnessing a crime can have a deep emotional effect, a fact to which Karen attested:

I was at an ice cream van when a guy held it up with a sawn-off shotgun. It was the most frightening experience of my life. I didn't know who he was but he would know me forever. He had a mask and a sawn-off shotgun which I thought was a bit much. He actually nudged me and screamed 'move'. The guys in the ice cream van were giving him everything they could get. They never, ever got the Polis. I was ill for days and every man I looked at, I thought was him.

It is likely that overcrowding and drunkenness contributed to an increase in the late nineteenth century in violence against women and children, but most went, and goes, unreported. It was not until 1898 that an assault by a husband on his wife was changed from a breach of the peace or petty assault to the more serious category of a crime against the person.

In the past 200 years changes in living conditions, relations between rich and poor, and between men and women, have been reflected in shifting views of the causes of crime, the rights of victims, the possibilities of rehabilitation and the justness of punishments. Glasgow's reputation as a city of crime is at least as much due to the intensity of these views as to the underlying, though undeniable, realities.

CHAPTER 14

DANCING AT THE BARROWLAND

Glasgow literally swarms with cheap, low dancing places, where the youth of both sexes among the lower ranks of society meet regularly once or twice a week, to dance, drink and enjoy themselves.

North British Daily Mail, Monday, 11 March 1872

Dancing has long been a popular activity in Glasgow. This chapter looks at the popularity of dancing in the city from ballroom dancing to discotheques, focusing on the Barrowland Ballroom.

The first purpose-built place for dancing was the Assembly Room in the Tontine Buildings which was funded by the Tobacco Lords in 1796. Only the wealthy could afford to dance there. By the 1920s, Glasgow had 11 ballrooms which was more than anywhere else in Britain; London, by contrast, only had three ballrooms at this time. With up to 70 other dance halls in the city, everyone was able to enjoy dancing, as Betty Knox (born 1922) recalled:

Och, they came in their thousands. Glasgow was the city of ballroom dancers in these days. We were really interested in ballroom dancing. Some of the finest ballrooms in the world were in Glasgow.

In the big ballrooms dress was formal and dance steps were regulated. People took lessons and watched the exhibition dancers who were employed by the bigger dance halls. The bigger dance halls also had resident bands.

You would graduate from the local hall to the Tower. Then from the Tower you would graduate to, it was called the Waldorf, and then it was called the Locarno, and then it was called Tiffany's. These were the dancing years, of course.

William Brown (born 1914,
talking about dancing in the 1930s)

On a Saturday night you got the Saturday night's *Times*. You'd all the dance halls on one page. 'Where'll we go tonight?' Maybe go to Dixon's Halls, or maybe to Govan Halls. Great choice of dance halls. Take your pick. The Tower – all these places. In that era if you couldn't dance you were ... a wallflower you know.'

Sam Watt (born 1919)

At formal dances people were given cards with the list of dances for that evening. Men and women could book dances with each other by writing their name beside their chosen dance. Women wore their best dresses, men suits and ties. Margaret Suttie (born 1922)

used to stand for hours ironing them all. Because the dress I had was chiffon and it had organdie frills all around the bottom. Oh, when I think of the hours I stood ironing that thing!

The Barrowland Ballroom, which opened on Christmas Eve 1934, was less posh than some of the other big dance halls but could hold over 2,000 people. For generations the Barrowland was a popular place to go dancing. It was one of the few places in Glasgow where new dances such as the Jitterbug were allowed. It stayed open during World War Two when the dress code was relaxed to allow the forces to wear their uniforms. The neon sign was taken down during the war years when it was mentioned by Lord Haw Haw in his radio broadcasts from Nazi Germany. He said that German planes were using it to navigate by.

People took their dancing very seriously. During the 1960s and '70s competition dances were held regularly at the Barrowland. The winners had to choose which box to open. It was based on the popular television show *Take Your Pick*. Cash prizes of up to £100 could be won if the winner chose the right box.

John and Sally McGowan (left) and friends, c. 1970.

LOVE AND ROMANCIN'

It was the in thing. If a girl was looking for a boy then that was the place to go and vice versa.

People went to the Barrowland because they enjoyed dancing, but it was also a way for men and women to meet each other. Staff at the Barrowland tried to ensure that everyone was given the chance to dance. Bandleader Billy MacGregor introduced 'Register Dancing'. As each woman came in she was given a book of tickets which she could give to a man she wished to dance with. The more tickets a man collected the more entries he got in the prize draw.

There were wallflowers. We used to talk to them, obviously they have paid their money and are entitled to enjoy themselves. Whether they are ugly or beautiful makes no difference. They are there. We would dance at the side with them 'til the ice is broke and as we knew most of the people we would say, 'Oh give them a turn. There's a lumber for you.'

John McGowan, who started work as a bouncer in 1967 and went on to become assistant manager and catering manager

The young ladies stood up one side of the hall and the men stood up on the other and at the first beat of the drum you ran over and got a hold. The procedure for dancing was stereotyped in all dance halls at that time. The lassies took one side of the hall and the aspirants to love took the other side.

William Brown (born 1914)

As well as having a reputation for love and romancing the Barrowland also had a reputation for gang violence. One woman remembers having to 'sneak out so that your mum didn't know where you were going as it was taboo then'. During the 1950s and '60s there were fights most nights between rival gangs. Men were searched and weapons taken from them were removed by the police every

Sketch of Billy MacGregor, 'King Showman'. Billy MacGregor led the Gaybirds, the Barrowland's resident band for over 30 years. He had been the drummer in the first band to open the ballroom in 1934. At the beginning of World War Two he took over the Gaybirds.

three months. John McGowan was paid 12/6 a night for his job as a bouncer in the late 1960s:

In those days it was rough and tough. We got all the gangs from Bridgeton, the Gorbals and the Calton but you got to know the ones you had to keep an eye on. If you were pally with some of them they kind of kept control of the ones who were in their gang. You had to be pretty fit to be a bouncer in the Barrowland but to be a good bouncer you need a good tongue because you talk your way out of trouble. We had a metal cabinet in the main office and there were four drawers in it and each and every one of these drawers was full of knives, bayonets, dummy guns. We had to take them off people at night. They were bringing in swords. Everything.

The Barrowland was run by very few staff with bouncers operating a strict door policy to help prevent violence. Men were searched for weapons and drink (the Barrowland was not licensed until 1973). Women were not searched and could smuggle knives and drink in in their handbags. McGowan recalled:

There were 18 bouncers, four assistant managers and a manager. That is 20 people to look after 2,000 people and 2,000 people jammed into a dance hall was a lot of people in one area. On a Friday night the queue would form up the Gallowgate, up Gibson Street along Moncur Street which is the back of the Barras. It was like a square. This was the queue to get into the Barrowland.

Architect's drawing for the new Barrowland Ballroom which opened on Christmas Eve 1960. The previous building was destroyed by fire on 19 August 1958.

'King Showman' Billy MacGregor and the Gaybirds, the longest-serving resident band at the Barrowland, planned events to help keep a happy atmosphere. Jimmy Philips, who joined the band in 1956, said: 'Every night was a riot. There were some good musicians in the band but you couldn't play for laughing. Billy MacGregor was probably the greatest showman band leader that I ever worked with.'

John McGowan remembers carnival nights:

We had hatches under the ceiling and we used to fill them up with balloons. Billy MacGregor would shout, 'It's carnival time,' and we had to release the balloons. It was amazing how people changed from being grumpy to being happy. It was unbelievable. It helped to control the trouble. The bursting of balloons would go on for about three quarters of an hour and we never had any trouble because people were that busy bursting balloons that they did not want to fight.

Dance floor of the Barrowland Ballroom when it re-opened after the fire in 1960.

When the Barrowland Ballroom was destroyed by fire on 19 August 1958, all of the band's instruments and music were destroyed, but director Sam McIver replaced the instruments and gave all the musicians other work until the Barrowland opened again. Jimmy Philips became a bookkeeper during this time. The 1949 film *Floodtide* featured the Gaybirds and starred actors Jimmy Logan, Rhona Anderson and Gordon Jackson.

As well as having a resident dance band, major big bands would make guest appearances. Singer Lena Martell also started her career singing with the Gaybirds at the Barrowland in the early 1960s.

After the Barrowland became licensed for over 21s only attendances dropped to only three to four hundred people a night, but the Barrowland Ballroom was already in decline having never recovered from the Bible John murders in the 1960s. Bible John murdered three women he met at the Barrowland. He was given that name because he was overheard quoting from the Bible. John McGowan said:

What ruined the Barrowland was the Bible John murders. We had police everywhere as if they were punters. You always heard the girls going ouch as they stood on their feet. They had probably never been to the dancing in their life. That was the downfall of it. Bible John was only the seed.

Today, the Barrowland is used as a venue for rock bands although there are over 40 nightclubs and discos in Glasgow with specialist clubs for single people, gays and lesbians and older people. Many clubs hold nostalgic nights which play music from the 1960s and 1970s. New clubs become the 'in place' to

Teddy Desmond's Symphonic Syncopaters pose for a publicity shot outside of the Palais de Dance, c. 1950.

go for a short while, but the enduring popularity of the Barrowland Ballroom ensures its place in Glasgow's history.

Couples dancing in the Calton, 1976 photograph by J.G.Gillies.

ABOVE

Glasgow Fair, the Saltmarket, 1825.

LEFT

Crowds of holidaymakers at Central Station, Glasgow Fair, c. 1925/26.

CHAPTER 15

DOON THE WATTER

Nine times out of ten it was raining. We were washed oot and washed back.

George Telfer (born 1920s)

Many Glaswegians take their holidays during the Fair Fortnight, which is the last two weeks in July. From the late nineteenth century until the 1950s only the very poorest people would spend the whole Fair Fortnight in Glasgow. The most popular holiday resorts were towns 'doon the watter' on the Clyde such as Rothesay (on the Isle of Bute), Dunoon and Largs. This chapter looks at how the Glasgow Fair developed, and the importance of memories of 'going doon the watter' for generations of Glaswegians.

The Fair Fortnight got its name from the fair which was held in Glasgow from *c.* 1190. It began on 7 July, the anniversary of the dedication of the cathedral, and ran for one week, though this was changed informally over the centuries so that the second Monday of July became Fair Monday. The fair was held at the top of the High Street for many centuries and then moved to various locations on the banks of the Clyde, mostly in the Stockwell Street area. Up to the end of the eighteenth century the fair was a huge market where cattle were bought and sold. When the new cattle market was opened in Graham Street in 1818 a new type of fair, involving sideshows, sprang up at the west end of Glasgow Green. The Victorian council ended the disreputable entertainments on the Green, and the sideshows moved to Veinegar Hill. Today a fair is held on Glasgow Green but it is now children's events and

sideshows, but the real fair for most Glaswegians involved going 'doon the watter'.

The advent of the steamboat in the early nineteenth century and railways from the 1830s meant that people could more easily travel out of the polluted industrial city to where the air was fresh. Competition between the paddle steamers and rail companies to places such as Greenock, Wemyss Bay and Ardrossan kept rail and boat fares along the Clyde amongst the lowest in Europe. Before paid holidays, when factories closed down during the fair, workers lost wages. People had to save up to cover the period without earnings.

Whole families and neighbours or even half the street would go away together. Sometimes the mother and children went first and the father would join them at the weekend, as Mrs Grace McDonald recalled:

> We had the house each year for two or three weeks but my father only had one week's holiday. Needless to say hordes of relatives would come down the first week to take up the vacant place.

This mass exodus from Glasgow resulted in queues of people trying to leave the city. In the 1920s the steamer took five and a half hours from the Broomielaw to Rothesay, and it cost more to have a seat on the deck. Bands played and people danced. The steamers were licensed to, sell alcohol although in 1882 an Act of Parliament stopped steamers from selling alcohol on a Sunday. It was faster to go by train to Gourock or Wemyss Bay, but it cost more. Rita Gentle (born 1920s) remembers waiting to leave from Central Station in the 1950s and recalls that 'the queues were unbelievable – half way down Argyle Street. Everyone was going doon the watter. The queues were horrendous, full of greetin' weans and laughing weans.'

Many people recall that Glasgow was like a ghost town during this time, with the holiday resorts full of Glasgow folk:

> *The overcrowding which takes place in coast towns such as Rothesay is scarcely to be believed. One day a typical Glasgow matron appeared before a Rothesay landlady and asked if she had apartments to let, and got an answer in the affirmative. 'Then,' said the Glasgow lady, 'I need five beds.' 'What!' said the landlady. 'Thirty folk; you're no comin' into ma hoose.'*
>
> G.G. Millar, *What'll the Folk Think*

Not all of the landlords welcomed Glaswegians:

> *The landlord sat at the outside toilet guarding his chickens because he thought all the people from Glasgow were going to kill his chickens and eat them. No way would the girls go into that toilet so we used the bucket in the bedroom.*
>
> *May Hutton*

From the 1960s cheap flights meant that increasing numbers of people could afford their holidays abroad and today the Clyde holiday resorts rely on day trippers. The *Waverley*, the last sea-going paddle steamer in the world, travels doon the watter during the summer months. The main difference noticed by passengers sailing down the Clyde today is the silence.

> *It is much quieter. It was all shipyards, the noise of the rivets and the welders all the way down. The industry is all away. It is more scenic now though.*

Crowded boats at the Broomielaw, Glasgow, c. 1920 (copyright Glasgow City Archives).

"IN THE GOOD OLD SUMMER TIME"

On the beach, Helensburgh, c. 1910.

Waiting for boats, Millport, c. 1910.

Staff of a typical Buttercup Dairy pose outside the shop, c. 1940s.

CHAPTER 16

THE BUTTERCUP DAIRY

Do you like Butter? Yes if it's Buttercup.

The Buttercup Dairy Company was a family business started by Andrew Ewing *c.* 1909. He opened his first shop in Lochgelly, Fife, before moving to Edinburgh. The headquarters were at Easter Road, Edinburgh. By the time he sold the company in 1949 he had over 400 shops. Half of these were on the west coast of Scotland.

There were Buttercup dairies all over Glasgow: two in the Great Western Road, three in Maryhill Road, New City Road, Garscube Road, Gourley Street and St Enoch's Square. The original Buttercup Dairy fittings in the People's Palace display come from the shop at 647 Great Western Road.

At first Mr Ewing only sold seven items in his shops – tea, margarine, butter, cream, eggs, condensed milk and cooking fat. The tea was imported and sold under the Buttercup label. The cream came fresh every morning from Pollock creamery. In the 1920s it was sold in Buttercup stoneware jars and later on in waxed paper cups. Eggs came from Mr Ewing's farm or were imported from Denmark. By 1948, the time of the People's Palace display, tinned and other products were sold.

Shortly before the Second World War Mr Ewing's nephew introduced self-service into the Buttercup dairies. He had seen this method of shopping in Canada. Shelves were fitted on all sides of the shops and customers picked their own goods and brought them to the counter. Only butter was sold from behind the counter. Butter was sold in bags with the slogan 'Do you like Butter? Yes, if it's Buttercup.'

Mr Ewing was very religious. All eggs laid by his hens on a Sunday were donated to hospitals in Edinburgh. He was strict with his staff, expecting them to follow the Buttercup Commandments, and in the 1920s sent his assistants a letter urging them not to bob their hair, quoting from St Paul's first letter to the Corinthians, which calls a woman's hair her 'crowning glory'.

In the 1920s assistants worked from 8 a.m. until 7 p.m. six days a week, with a half day on a Tuesday. The weekly wage was 9/- (45p). The girls had to wear long white bibbed aprons and stiff cuffs. These had to be fresh daily and the girls were expected to do their own laundry. Staff were sometimes rewarded for good work. Miss Manson, an assistant at New City Road from 1921, was given a reward of two pounds for having a well-dressed window.

When the Buttercup Dairy was sold in 1949 staff in the 400 shops were given the opportunity to buy them. Miss Manson, who began working for the company in 1921, bought the Great Western Road shop. She ran this until August 1975.

SOME OF THE BUTTERCUP
DAIRY COMMANDMENTS

It is always worth while to serve with a smile.

A parcel neatly and firmly wrapped will bring customers back.

Cleanliness in handling food cannot achieve anything but good.

Where the staff is bright and cheery, business will be brisk and bright, never dreary.

Economise in light, paper boxes and string – be careful – do not waste anything.

If your customer says it's white it's white, for your customer is always right.

Photograph of a Great Western Road branch, c. 1940s (photograph copyright, Glasgow City Archives).

THE PEOPLE'S PALACE BOOK OF GLASGOW

MRS CARMICHAEL'S RANT

Mrs Carmichael's Rant is an imaginary tirade which reflects the pressures shopkeepers would have been under in a Buttercup Dairy shop in 1948, the year before Mr Ewing sold the company. Mrs Carmichael, who runs the dairy for Mr Ewing, is having a bad day. Although the war is over some products are still rationed and people are complaining about the shortages. Mrs Carmichael is also concerned about rumours that the shop is to be sold. She is called out from the back by a customer ringing the bell.

(Visitor rings bell for attention)

Would ye gie that bell a rest. Ah'm no deaf. Oh it's you, is it? I thought it wiz yon young hooligans frae Greenhead Street. And what wi' the day ah've had. Nothin' but, 'Hey Missus goat ony sweeties.' And eggs. They're all wantin' eggs! Well I ask ye. There's none knows better than masel' that the war's ower. What wi' him through there limpin' about like to put the hens aff layin'. But in they come wi' their coupons. Think just cos it's got a fancy stamp that I can just magic the stuff. Like I've had it through the back all along and widnae sell it. Sell it! Dinny think ah widnee sell the paper aff the walls if I thought it wid pass as sliced breed.

But just about a'body's had it hard. I hid that wee Sadie Thompson in this morning wi' a line and a shoppin' bag bigger than hersel'. That's twa month noo her ma's been bad wi' the cough. Like as no, she'll no mak it. No eleven year old and that wean's running the hoose. Out doing the stairs she wiz and it wiz hardly daylight. *(Sighs)* Ah! we dinny let them stay weans long these days.

(Toughens up again, embarrassed by momentary lapse)

Some o' those weans though! See that Jimmy Clegg! (*Raises voice and shocks visitor*) 'One more time, Jimmy Clegg,' says I, 'Ah catch you wi' yer haund o'er that counter and it's the Polis fur ye.' Anyway whit wiz it ye wanted? Some o' that new margarine and four slices o' bacon. That'll be yer rations. Twa fur yerrsel' and twa fur Wullie. That was an afae business yon. Ah'm no surprised your Wullie's ta'en bad over it. But at least ye've got a hoose. Oh! ye were gonny tell me about that new family next close but one. Where did ye say they were frae. Poland is it. Big faimily eh. Well that canny be bad fur business. That's if we're still here and me that's that saft half o' them round here hardly pays ony way.

(Drops voice to conspiratorial whisper)

Sorry that I am, Ah've had to say nay mair credit, Mrs Leckie, 'til I see some change. Puir woman's got that there's nothin' left but the claithes on her back, and ye know fine she gangs hungry tae see the weans fed.

(Voice gains strength again)

Aye who knows where ony o' us wull be this time next year if what we hear is true. Aye mind ye, it's just a rumour the noo. Ah think they mak it up as they go along. Still, if Mr Ewing is fur sellin up I daresae we'll know soon enough what wi' 200 shops in the Glesga area. That you then? Gi'es o'er yer bag. Tell ye whit ah'll come by the nicht efter Ah've dropped in on poor auld Mrs Mackie wi' her messages and we can tak the time tae ha' a proper chat. Aye, Aye, I see ye, Mrs O'Hagan. I'm no blind. What's it the day? Eggs is it?

Partick steamie, 1950s (photograph by Alf Daniel).

THE PEOPLE'S PALACE BOOK OF GLASGOW

CHAPTER 17

THE TALK O' THE STEAMIE

The first public wash-house in Glasgow was on Glasgow Green from 1732–1820 and the people of the city continue to have the right to hang their washing here to this day. The Greenhead Public Baths and Washing House were opened in 1878 in Bridgeton by the corporation which was concerned about the lack of running water in people's houses. Facilities were provided for people to wash both themselves and their laundry at public baths and wash-houses, or steamies as they were known, all over the city, before people had their own washing machines.

Washing at the steamie was extremely hard physical work, carried out by women. Every week they took their family's dirty washing to the steamie in prams, tin baths and baskets. When they got there they sorted the white items and the coloureds into different piles, and then washed them separately by hand in the big tubs or the boilers. Afterwards they had to shift all the wet washing either onto the drying racks in the steamie or take it home to their own back green to dry. May Hutton recalled:

You got up and stripped the beds and got all the dirty washing. You had the big zinc bath and packed it all with the dirty washing. You kept your nappies separate because they were getting boiled separate. Your soap powder and washing board was tied up with string round the bath and onto your pram and

away round the steamie with your wellies. You had your wellies because the floor was soaking. We didn't have machines when I used the steamie, you did your hand wash and your boiling stuff was boiling away. You had dryers. Once the first lot was done you put them in the wringer and then it was a big roll, like steel rods that pulled out, and you dried your blankets and your washing in that.

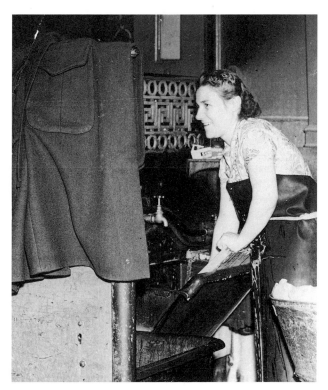

Whiteinch Wash-house.

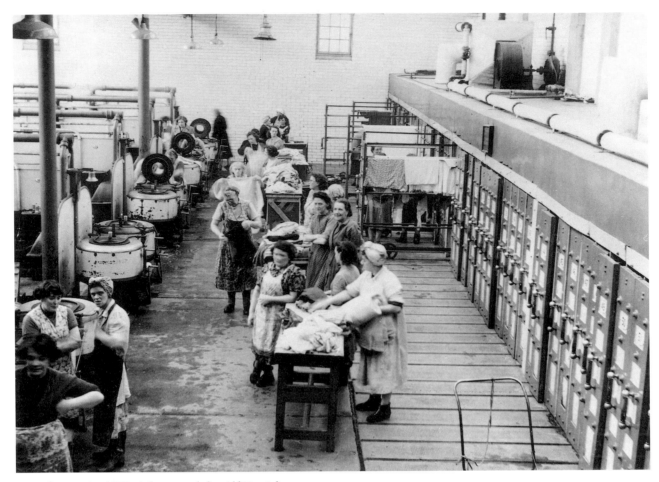

Partick steamie, 1950s (photograph by Alf Daniel).

Launderette, 1950s (photograph by Alf Daniel).

The positive side of going to the steamie was that it was the place for a good gossip and a chance to catch up with your friends. The nostalgia felt by many women for this sociable female world is portrayed with great humour and humanity in Tony Roper's play *The Steamie*. May Hutton said:

> It was great! You got all the gossip – who went away with the man doon the street and who didn't pay the coalman!

Partick steamie continued to operate as a steamie until 1982, when it was modernised with electric machines, and it finally shut in 1992. Steamies closed down as more people either could afford to have their own washing machines at home or used the launderette with its more efficient washing machines and dryers.

CHAPTER 18

VISIONS OF THE CITY

There is not one Glasgow, and no one history of Glasgow – the city will have seemed very different depending on where any individual was in relation to the structures of political and financial power which have shaped life in the city. The museum displays present four visions – of the kind of place Glasgow is and should be, which have guided people's behaviour over the past 250 years.

A centrepiece of the People's Palace displays is the vision of painter Ken Currie, whose epic paintings represent a radical socialist view of the history of the city. Another account of the people's visions uses the museum's collection of banners, trade symbols, co-operative and suffragette material to show how they, led by politicians such as the socialists John Maclean and James Maxton, have struggled against appalling living and working conditions, armed with a vision of a fairer and better life for themselves and their families. A competing vision is that of capitalists, who have seen Glasgow as a place to make money, a place of business opportunity and the centre of world markets. Somewhere between these are the civic visions of members of the corporation or council who tried to develop and promote Glasgow as a great city in which to live and to work.

These visions, and the actions they inspire, influence the way the city is run in terms of

VOTE FOR MAXTON
AND SAVE THE CHILDREN.

James Maxton (1885–1946), Independent Labour Party MP for Bridgeton, 1922. James Maxton was one of the Clydesiders elected to Parliament in 1922. A teacher himself, he also fought for improved conditions for teachers and campaigned for the under privileged children.

Ken Currie at work.

power, politics and money. All of us who live in Glasgow are affected by these different ideas, whether we run a business or are unemployed because our skills are no longer needed; whether we provide the street lighting or benefit from it after dark; or whether we campaign actively for a political party or are able to enjoy the right to vote won by campaigners.

A Radical Socialist Vision: the People's Palace History Paintings

To mark the 1987 bicentenary of the massacre of Glasgow's Calton weavers, Scotland's first trade union martyrs, the artist Ken Currie was commissioned by the People's Palace to produce a series of eight paintings for the dome on the top floor of the building. The paintings provide an interpretation of Glasgow's political and labour history.

The paintings were funded by the bequest of Tommy Chambers, who died in 1984. Trained as a railway engineer, he became unemployed in 1922 and then took up cycling as a member of the Kinning Park Socialist Cycling Club. The paintings are a fitting tribute to this lifelong socialist and the other unsung heroes and heroines of the labour movement.

At the time of painting, Ken Currie was a Marxist and he represented the struggle of the working classes according to the Marxist principle of history as class conflict. He wanted to 'represent a cycle of images that showed the ebb and flow of an emergent mass movement, where the real heroines and heroes were the many unknown working-class Scots who fought so selflessly for their rights'.

The cycle of paintings begins in 1787 and ends with a vision of the future. The late eighteenth century was a period of much radical action. On 3 September 1787 weavers in the Calton area of Glasgow had been on strike for more than 12

Demonstration against the threatened closure of Glasgow shipyards, 1971. When the government tried to close the Upper Clyde Shipbuilders, instead of a strike the unions organised a different type of industrial protest: a work-in.

Red Clydeside: the Forty Hours' Strike demonstration, 1919.

In January 1919 the red flag of Socialism flew in George Square when Glasgow workers gathered to campaign for a 40-hour working week. The government feared revolution and had the troops ready in case of a riot. Many Labour leaders such as Emmanuel Shinwell, David Kirkwood and William Gallacher were arrested. What happened in 1919 is seen as a major event in the history of Glasgow workers.

weeks in protest at their wages being cut to starvation level. The military were called in by the Lord Provost to quell a demonstration and they shot dead six weavers and injured many others.

At the time of the French Revolution in 1789 radicals in Scotland were also campaigning for the rights of the ordinary people. The government was concerned that workers joining together in trade unions might pose a revolutionary threat. In 1797 'Combinations', or trade unions, were banned so any union activity had to be held in secret. As the nineteenth century progressed, unions were made legal, and members continued to campaign for better lives for themselves. Huge demonstrations took place in Glasgow prior to

the Reform Bills of 1832, 1868 and 1884, when sometimes as many as 250,000 tradespeople gathered together to march through the streets in support of parliamentary reform. They carried banners and symbols of their trades, such as ships and kilns and beehives, which represented industry. This long struggle to get all adults the vote on equal terms did not finally succeed until 1929.

Glasgow socialists always saw themselves in a world context and many people were inspired by the writings of Karl Marx's communist manifesto. Socialism was seen as a way of rescuing society from the horrors of poverty and deprivation. In 1888 the Scottish Labour Party was formed, and in 1893 the Independent Labour Party was founded. John Maclean, pioneering socialist, was appointed by Lenin as Scottish consul to the Bolshevik government in Russia in 1918. Socialists not only campaigned for the political rights of the workers, but also developed clubs such as the Clarion Cyclists and scouts and choirs, encouraging more healthy and fulfilling lifestyles.

During the early part of the twentieth century Glasgow became known as Red Clydeside and was a centre of socialist political campaigns. These included a Rent Strike in 1915–16 where tenants, mostly women whose husbands were fighting in the First World War, refused to pay increased rents and succeeded in restricting the increases. The most famous demonstration of this period was the Forty Hours' Strike in 1919 when a huge gathering of workers called for shorter working hours. The red flag was flown in George Square and the government, fearing a revolution, brought in troops.

In 1971, when the government tried to close the Upper Clyde Shipbuilders, instead of organising a strike the unions organised a different type of political action, a 'work in'. To prove that shipbuilding was still a going concern the workers continued to build despite the attempted closure of the yard. This dispute symbolised the decline in shipbuilding in Glasgow and was supported by many unions.

The final painting portrays a vision of the light of socialism illuminating the future, with men and women working together to bring about a more equal society.

People's Visions

UNITY IS STRENGTH

Down with Class rule!
Down with the rule of brute force!
Down with war!
Up with the peaceful rule of the people!

An appeal to the working class, Keir Hardie and Arthur Henderson, 1914

Many objects from the Museum's collections are included in the Ken Currie paintings such as trades union banners and the symbols carried by trades in the great nineteenth-century demonstrations. These and other objects are included in the People's Visions display, which tells the story of communal action and left wing politics through which people tried to achieve their vision of a better society. People in Glasgow have gathered together to try to improve their lives, fighting for the right to vote and for a better and fairer society. By working together through trade unions, in political parties and the co-operative movement, the people have gained a stronger voice and a greater power to change things.

Anna Munro, suffragette who campaigned for the vote for women in Glasgow.

WORKERS UNITE

Workers have gathered together in trade unions since the 1700s to negotiate with their employers to improve their pay and working conditions. They often protested by withholding their labour and going on strike. Different trades have had their own unions, but when one union was in dispute with their employers others would often support them. They have marched through the city and had demonstrations in Glasgow Green and George Square to show the solidarity of the workers, both during disputes and in celebration on May Day.

THE STRUGGLE FOR THE VOTE

Today we take it for granted that we have the right to vote, whether we are women or men, rich or poor, black or white, Catholic or Protestant. However, it was not until 1918 that all men over 21 and women over 30 were granted the vote. Women over 21 were only given the vote in 1928. People have struggled for this right to vote and elect the government of their choice. They have organised huge demonstrations and campaigns to put their point forward. In fighting laws which they thought unjust some people have broken the law and have gone to prison for their beliefs.

PARTY POLITICS

Many political parties have represented the people of Glasgow including the Labour Party, the Independent Labour Party, the Liberals, the Communist Party, the Scottish National Party and the Conservatives. Banners from both the Conservatives and the ILP have been preserved in the collection. Many politicians have not only

Anti-poll tax banner.
Glasgow was a centre of opposition to the poll tax, a tax on every adult which was introduced by
the Conservative government in 1989 in Scotland, a year before England. The unfairness of the tax
and inability of people to pay inspired a massive non-payment campaign led by Tommy Sheridan.
The Anti-Poll Tax campaign eventually caused the tax to be abolished in 1992.

supported local issues on the streets of Glasgow but have contributed to the British political scene, as founders of parties, MPs, party leaders and prime ministers. Since the 1930s the Glasgow political scene has been dominated by the Labour Party.

GLASGOW PROTESTS

Glasgow people have protested over issues such as rents and nuclear weapons, and taxes such as the poll tax. The campaign against the poll tax in 1987 aroused high passions in Glasgow and striking posters by Central Designs/Cranhill Arts are on display in the museum.

> We appeal to all non-payers to stand firm and get involved in the campaign and we appeal to those who are paying to stop paying and join the campaign. Remember this Poll Tax is evil, unjust and immoral. Don't condone it by paying it, defeat it by making it unworkable and uncollectable. The more non-payers the quicker the whole thing will collapse around Thatcher's ears.
>
> *Strathclyde Anti-Poll Tax Federation leaflet*

THE CO-OP

The Co-operative movement promoted a vision of a more equal and sharing society. Members could not only buy high-quality goods at competitive prices made at the Shieldhall factory, they also got a share of the profits, through the 'divi' or dividend. Co-op services ranged from grocery stores to funeral arrangements and the boast was that 'the Co' looked after its members from the cradle to the grave. The Co-operative women's guilds were popular meeting places for women, for many of whom they provided an initiation into political activity.

TEMPERANCE

One item the Co-op shops did not sell was alcohol because of the damage alcohol abuse did to people's lives. The Co-op, along with other labour organisations such as the Independent Labour Party and the Glasgow Trades Council, supported the temperance movement which encouraged people to drink less. Some groups within it believed in complete prohibition and had a vision of an alcohol-free city. Glasgow's famous tea rooms, such as those owned by Miss Cranston and designed by Charles Rennie Mackintosh, were in part an attempt to provide alcohol-free places for people to meet and relax. Temperance banners and tea sets are featured in the displays, as are artefacts relating to the consumption of alcohol (see the chapter entitled The Bevvy).

Capitalist Visions

MONEY MAKES THE WORLD GO ROUND

> To raise the living standards and quality of life of all in our society more wealth must be created.
>
> It is the job of business to create wealth. To survive, thrive and grow we need to match and, where possible, to surpass, the best in the world.
>
> *The Scottish Business Agenda, CBI Scotland, 1995*

For some people Glasgow has been a good place to make money, both on a large and small scale. Merchants, manufacturers and business people have made huge fortunes through activities ranging from trading in tobacco to building ships, from making carpets to creating national hotel chains. Banks and insurance companies were set up to service the trading and manufacturing, and shops to provide for the growing population.

Some built on the family businesses they inherited, but many were self-made men, starting like Thomas Lipton, grocer extraordinaire, with one small shop and expanding to create international business empires. In the process he brought cheaper groceries to the people of Glasgow, and Britain. Sir Thomas Lipton's log asserts:

The Glasgow Necropolis, 1866.
The Necropolis, or 'city of the dead', was opened beside the cathedral in 1833 and is the burial place of many famous wealthy Glasgow capitalists. As well as reflecting the love and respect of those left behind, the large tombs and monuments show off the families' wealth and importance.

Reo Stakis, 1970s, by Alasdair Gray. Originally from Cyprus, Reo Stakis became a successful Glasgow businessman, owning hotels and restaurants.

Portrait of Sir Thomas Lipton from one of his many grocery shops, 1890s.

I kept telling myself that if I could make eighteen pounds by selling a few hams, I could make hundreds by selling a thousand of them. The operation was the same; the quantities didn't matter.

Glasgow capitalists were usually involved in many more businesses than that in which they made their initial fortune, and most were closely linked through complex networks of partnerships, directorships, family ties and membership of organisations such as the Trades and Merchants Houses, the volunteer regiments, churches, charities, the freemasons and the political and literary clubs. From the seventeenth to the nineteenth centuries, by holding positions of power in the town and on the town council, they ensured that they ran Glasgow in their own interests.

GOOD WORKS AND GRANDEUR

Glasgow merchants and industrialists were keen to display their wealth for all to see, and many of the most beautiful objects in Glasgow museums – and some of the buildings – were created, commissioned or purchased by them. The eighteenth-century Tobacco Lords paraded through Glasgow Cross in red frock coats, powdered wigs and cocked hats, and travelled in sedan chairs. Businessmen of later ages exchanged these for top hats and limousines. Large houses have always been a sign of wealth, whether the impressive town houses such as that of Tobacco Lord, William Cunninghame (now the Gallery of Modern Art) in Queen Street or a villa on the Clyde coast. This conspicuous display of wealth was not just for show. More money could be raised if investors had faith in their existing wealth, and clients were lavishly entertained in their mansions and luxurious steam yachts in order to gain their custom.

Many Glasgow capitalists, whether from religious belief, a concern for humanity, a love of the city or the vanity of wishing their name to live on for posterity, have put some of their

fortunes back into the city. They have provided parks such as Cathkin Braes Park and Govan's Elder Park. Stirling's Library, housed for a while in William Cunninghame's mansion, and the Mitchell Library were donated by rich merchants, and important art collections were given to the city by Archibald MacLellan, Sir William Burrell, the family of Sir James Reid and many others. The city's hospitals and universities have received a great many gifts, and charitable foundations were set up to look after the less fortunate of Glasgow's citizens. Today the Trades and Merchants Houses continue this charitable tradition.

Burrell Collection, opened 1983.
Sir William and Lady Constance Burrell donated their art collections to Glasgow in 1944. Collecting art was one way of enjoying your riches, and the quality and size of the Burrell Collection means that the name will live on for posterity.

Trams outside Kelvingrove Museum and Art Gallery, 1950s (courtesy of J. M. McCorquodale).

When they were built in 1969 the Red Road flats were the tallest flats in Europe.

In 1888 Queen Victoria inaugurated the new Municipal Buildings, now the City Chambers, the centre of Glasgow's local authority administration.

Civic Visions

In Glasgow a citizen may live in a municipal house; he may walk along the municipal street, or ride on the municipal tramcar and watch the municipal dustcart collecting the refuse which is to be used to fertilise the municipal farm. Then he may turn into the municipal market, buy a steak from an animal killed in the municipal slaughterhouse, and cook it by the municipal gas stove. For his recreation he can choose among municipal libraries, municipal art galleries, and municipal telephone, or he may be taken to the municipal hospital in the municipal ambulance by a municipal policeman. Should he be so unfortunate as to get on fire, he will be put out by the municipal fireman,

Corporation of Glasgow inspection of Gorbals Waterworks, 27 September 1899.

Lollipop man seeing schoolchildren safely across the road, 1950s (by H. B. Coventry).

using municipal water, after which he will, perhaps, forego the enjoyment of using the municipal bath, though he may find it necessary to get a new suit in the municipal old clothes market.

Fortnightly Review, 1903

The council in Glasgow provides a wide range of mostly free services, paid for by local taxes and government grants. The council was originally run by the merchants and craftsmen of the town; now both female and male councillors are elected by all the people in Glasgow, to represent their local areas. The councillors have always had visions of making Glasgow the biggest and best. Glasgow has had many 'firsts', including the world's first municipal tram system (1894); the first telephone exchange in the country (1897); and the tallest blocks of flats in Europe, Red Road Flats (completed 1969).

In the 1980s and 1990s Glasgow's Labour Council has worked closely with business and government agencies such as the Glasgow Development Association to regenerate the city, looking for common ground between the people's, civic and capitalist visions in order to help create jobs and to relieve poverty:

As Glasgow moves towards the twenty-first century, it will prosper and flourish as an international city where people will choose to live, learn, work and play.

A City Vision for Glasgow, 1995.

VISION OF A SAFE AND HEALTHY CITY

Glasgow has been notorious as one of the most unhealthy cities in Europe, and it is still the poorest and most unhealthy city in Britain. Through the departments of water, environmental health, cleansing, housing and parks and recreation, the city has tried to improve living conditions and encourage healthier lifestyles. Council initiatives, including the introduction of a water supply from Loch Katrine in 1859, being the second largest provider of council housing in the world (after Hong Kong) and the current Healthy City project, continue to try to improve the well-being of the citizens.

By supplying everything from police and fire services to street lighting, the council has tried to make Glasgow a safe place for its people.

VISION OF A WELL SERVED CITY

The council has provided all sorts of services for the city from gas (1869–1948) and electricity (1893–1948) to public transport. The council influences the way the city looks and develops. This includes demolishing bad housing, preserving historic buildings and providing new roads and bridges.

Glasgow City Centre is the heart of West Central Scotland. The City has been a European City of Culture, is to be the City of Architecture and Design in 1999, and has the opportunity to build on past successes to become a leading city in an expanding Europe. For it to take that place, it will need a City Centre that is vibrant and attractive for all those people who will live, work, study, shop and relax in it.

Glasgow City Centre Millennium Plan, 1995

Marine Division, City of Glasgow Police, 1881.

VISION OF A CULTURAL CITY

Glasgow has long seen itself as a cultural centre, competing with other cities (especially Edinburgh) in the quality and energy of its cultural life. Many were surprised when Glasgow won the title of Cultural Capital of Europe in 1990, but this festival revealed the cultural wealth of the city.

> My council is determined that 1990 will be a year to remember for all Glaswegians. It will be a year of fun and entertainment with something to suit all tastes . . . Although we want to attract thousands of tourists and visitors whose spending power will bolster the city's economy, 1990 is primarily a festival for local people.
>
> *Councillor Pat Lally, Glasgow District Council*

The council not only runs the largest municipal museum service in Britain, has the largest public reference library in Europe (the Mitchell Library), it also runs its own theatres and concert halls and libraries and supports many other cultural events and organisations across the city.

Important Dates in Glasgow's Political and Economic History

1605
Merchants House established.

1707
Glasgow merchants build up trade with the colonies in tobacco, sugar and cotton.

1732
The public wash-house on Glasgow Green is opened.

1733
The town's hospital is built for the care of the poor.

1750
First bank in Glasgow opens, the Ship Bank.

1767
The Glasgow Weavers Society is formed, the first trade union in Glasgow.

1787
Calton weavers demonstrate against a cut in wages. Six men killed by the militia.

1790
The first public sewer (into the Clyde) is built.

1792
The radical Friends of the People organisation is set up in Glasgow, calling for equal representation in parliament.

1798
Charles Tennant establishes chemical works at St Rollox which becomes the largest chemical company in the world.

1799
The Anti-Combination Laws are passed, making trade unions illegal.

1800
The Police Commission is created to deal with scavenging, street lighting and law and order.

1806
The Glasgow Cotton Spinners Union is formed.

1820
The Glasgow Insurrection: 60,000 workers strike in support of parliamentary reform. John Baird and Andrew Hardie are arrested and later hanged for their part in the 'revolt'.

1824
Repeal of the Combination laws. Trade unions are no longer illegal.

1828
James Beaumont Neilson patents 'hot-blast' process for making iron.

1830
The Scottish Temperance Society is formed in Glasgow.

1831
100,000 people march on Glasgow Green in support of the Parliamentary Reform Bill.

1832
The first Reform Act (Scotland) is passed, giving 7,000 Glasgow men the right to vote. Glasgow has its own MPs for the first time since 1707.

1838
Five leaders of the Glasgow Cotton Spinners Union are sentenced to seven years' transportation after a strike and the union collapses as a result.

1839
James Templeton patents the chenille method of making carpets and opens factory in King Street.

1844
Glasgow Stock Exchange established.

1850
Walter Macfarlane opens Saracen Foundry, specialising in architectural ironwork.

1854
Archibald McLellan, coachbuilder, donates his art collection to the city.

1856
The city acquires the McLellan Galleries, the basis of the city's museum service.

1859
The first water from Loch Katrine reaches the city. John Anderson opens Royal Polytechnic Warehouse on Jamaica Street, Glasgow's first department store.

1863
The first Medical Officer of Health is appointed.

1866
The first municipal hospital, the fever hospital in Parliamentary Road, is opened.

1868
The Second Reform Act (Scotland) is passed, increasing Glasgow's electorate from 18,000 to over 47,000. The Scottish Co-operative Wholesale Society is established.

1869
The city takes over the manufacture and supply of gas.

1871
William Arroll establishes the Dalmarnock Iron Works. Thomas Lipton opens his first shop at 101 Stobcross Street.

1872
The Ballot Act introduces secret voting.

1873
The Glasgow School Board is formed to run the city schools.

1874
Stephen Mitchell, tobacco merchant, bequeaths his fortune to the city of Glasgow for the establishment of a large public library. Fraser & McLaren's department store opens.

1877
William Collins, publisher and advocate of temperance, is elected Lord Provost. The Mitchell Library is opened.

1878
The first municipal swimming baths and wash-house at Greenhead are opened.

1885
William and George Burrell take over control of their father's shipping company. Hugh Tennent begins brewing lager in Glasgow.

1886
William Pearce floats his shipyard on the stock exchange and renames it the Fairfield Shipbuilding and Engineering Company.

1887
William Beardmore takes control of Parkhead Forge.

1888
The council moves into the splendid new City Chambers in George Square. The first municipal houses in Saltmarket are built. The Scottish Labour Party is formed by Keir Hardie and R.B. Cunninghame Graham. Glasgow's first International Exhibition.

1890
The city takes over the manufacture and supply of electricity.

1894
The city takes over the tramway system. The Independent Labour Party is formed by Keir Hardie.

1895
William Collins, the publisher, dies. By this time his business employed 2,000 people and was one of the largest in the country.

1897
Thomas Lipton is knighted and floats his company on the stock exchange.

1898
The People's Palace opens.

1900–1906
The council runs the telephone service.

1901

The city takes over the new Art Gallery at Kelvingrove after the International Exhibition. The city opens its first lending library. Robert Smyth McColl and his brother open their first sweet shop in Albert Drive.

1906

Henry Campbell-Bannerman, a Glasgow textile merchant, becomes the first businessman to be elected Prime Minister.

1914–18

Glasgow businesses, especially Beardmore and Weirs, benefit greatly from supplying the war effort.

1915

The Rent Strike: 25,000 tenants refuse to pay their rents in protest over huge increases. Women play a major part in this struggle. The Clyde Engineers Strike: workers protest at new powers given to employers under war measures and the 'dilution' of their trades.

1916

Forward, a Socialist newspaper, is banned by the government. Peace campaigners John Maclean, Jimmy Maxton and James MacDougall are arrested for sedition and imprisoned.

1918

All men over 21 and women over 30 years of age are granted the vote.

1919

Forty-Hour Week Strike: huge demonstration in George Square, calling for a reduction in the working week, is baton charged by police. English troops with tanks are brought in by the government fearing revolution.

1920

For the first time, council elections are contested on party lines. National Rent Strike against the new Rent Act: 60,000 demonstrate on Glasgow Green.

1921

National Unemployed Workers Movement is formed. William Beardmore is created Lord Invernairn. By now he is the holder of over 20 directorships in steel and engineering companies.

1925

R. S. McColl is floated on the stock exchange. The company is valued at £350,000.

1927

The right of public assembly on Glasgow Green is revoked.

1928

William Beardmore loses control of his empire through bad debts, his businesses are rescued only by the intervention of the Bank of England. Women get the vote on the same basis as men.

1931

Sir Thomas Lipton dies, leaving his entire estate 'for the endowment or relief of the poor and destitute'.

1932

Right of public assembly on Glasgow Green is restored.

1933

The Labour Party gains control of the city council for the first time. R. S. McColl is sold to Cadbury's. The firm then employed 800 in its sweet factory and 180 shops.

1935

Hunger March in Glasgow.

1937

Apprentices strike for better pay and union rights.

1938

The pioneering Crookston Homes are built for the elderly.

1939–45

Glasgow businesses once again experience a boom in the supply of war materials.

1942

Reo Stakis, a Cypriot immigrant, establishes the Reo Stakis hotel chain as a public limited company.

1944

Sir William Burrell presents his art collection to the city of Glasgow.

1947

Langside College, the first further education college, is opened.

1948

Hugh Fraser floats his business on the stock exchange to form the 'House of Fraser'.

1959

Hugh Fraser purchases Harrods Ltd. The first CND march in Glasgow.

1960

Hugh Fraser establishes the Hugh Fraser Foundation for Charity with a £2.5 million endowment.

1966

Hugh Fraser dies. His retail empire includes 75 House of Fraser stores. In under twenty years he increased the group's turnover from £4 million to £99 million.

1970

The Kingston Bridge is opened.

1971–2

Upper Clyde Shipbuilders Work-in.

1975–96

The city council shares responsibility for public services with Strathclyde Regional Council.

1982

Health workers strike.

1983

Burrell Collection opens in Pollok Park.

1984-5

The Miners' Strike.

1985

The Scottish Exhibition and Conference Centre is opened on derelict dockland.

1987–92

Anti-poll tax demonstrations. Mass non-payment by Glasgow citizens. Tommy Sheridan establishes the All Britain Anti-Poll Tax Federation.

1988

4,500,000 people visit the Garden Festival.

1990

Glasgow is European City of Culture.
The Royal Concert Hall is opened during the year.

1995

Environmental campaigners stage tree-top protest against the extension of the M77 through Pollok Park.

1996

A new unitary Glasgow City Council is formed, and Strathclyde Regional council abolished. With a reduced tax base, the city suffers major cutbacks in services. Glasgow celebrates a Year of the Visual Arts to mark the centenary of Mackintosh's School of Art and the opening of the Gallery of Modern Art.

1998

Glasgow celebrates the centenary of the People's Palace.

1999

Glasgow is Arts Council of Great Britain City of Architecture and Design.

FURTHER READING

The Clyde – A Portrait of a River, Michael Moss, Canongate, 1997.

The Complete Patter, Michael Munro, Canongate, 1996.

Footsteps and Witnesses, Lesbian and Gay Life Stories from Scotland, edited by Bob Cant, Polygon, 1993.

Glasgow Vol. II: 1830 to 1912, edited by W. Hamish Fraser and Irene Maver, Manchester University Press, 1996.

The Glasgow Encyclopedia, Joe Fisher, Mainstream, 1994.

Glasgow and the Clyde at War, Paul Harris, Archive Publications, 1986.

Glasgow's Glasgow; The Words and the Stones, 1990.

Glasgow, Maurice Lindsay, Hale, 1989.

Parliamo Glasgow, Stanley Baxter, Omnibus, 1997.

The Hidden History of Glasgow's Women, Elspeth King, Mainstream, 1993.

The People's Palace & Glasgow Green, Elspeth King, Chambers, 1988.

The Third Statistical Account of Scotland, Glasgow, edited by J. Cunnison and J.B.S. Gilfillan, Collins, 1958.

Tongs ya bass (Part 1), R.G. MacCallum, New Glasgow Library, 1994.

Scotland Sober and Free, Elspeth King, Glasgow Museums, 1979.